MOMMY, I'M A GIRL!

MY ACCEPTANCE JOURNEY
MOTHERING A TRANSGENDER CHILD

TASHA KUXHAUSEN

This book is a memoir. It reflects the author's present recollections of experiences over time. For privacy reasons, some names, characteristics, locations, and dates may have been changed.

Published and distributed by Merack Publishing
San Diego, USA
www.merackpublishing.com

Library of Congress Control Number: 2023901176
Kuxhausen, Tasha

ISBN 978-1-957048-85-7 (Paperback)
ISBN 978-1-957048-86-4 (Hardcover)
ISBN 978-1-957048-87-1 (eBook)

For Elsa; my daughter, my hero

FOREWORD

Research supports the notion that young transgender children can have a valid and authentic understanding of their gender identity. Numerous studies have shown that gender identity develops early in life and can manifest as early as toddlerhood. Transgender children, even as young as three years old, can communicate a gender identity that is incongruent with their designated sex at birth. In recent years, the medical and psychological communities have recognized the importance of affirming and supporting the gender identities of transgender children. Additionally, the World Professional Association for Transgender Health (WPATH) acknowledges that gender identity can be reliably expressed by children, even at a young age.

Longitudinal studies have shown that transgender children who are supported in their gender identity experience improved mental health outcomes and well-being. Conversely, those who are not supported, or face rejection from their families or society, are more likely to experience negative mental health effects. While some may argue that young children may be influenced or confused, research suggests that transgender children's gender identities are consistent over time, and their understanding of their gender is a deeply ingrained aspect of their self-identity. It is crucial to trust and validate their experiences, as this contributes to their overall well-being and sense of self. It is essential to note that each child's journey is unique. Elsa's journey to authenticity is a beautiful example of the freedom that can be gained when one is allowed to be their true self.

As a gender-affirming therapist, I have worked with hundreds of families navigating the path with a transgender child. Pivotal to this experience is the knowledge that they are not alone, and others have walked this path before them. Tasha gives a raw, loving, and honest account of taking this journey with her own child, which will be invaluable to other families embarking on their own. Tasha's evolution from dread and anxiety to fierce advocacy and pride is sure to be one to inspire anyone who makes the choice to read this account of love, affirmation, and growth. Her willingness to share her experiences with vulnerability and authenticity is both courageous and crucial at this time in history. It is a testament to the power of storytelling and the profound impact it can have on others. Thank you to Elsa and her parents, who are willing to share their story to ignite change, challenge perceptions, and inspire others to embrace their own truths. Through their words, they have created a roadmap for healing, growth, and the unyielding power of love.

Darlene Tando, LCSW

CONTENTS

TO TASHA, ON MOTHER'S DAY
APRIL 30, 2016

Morning, warm shimmer
each moment the marveling
wonderous difficult joy
love, a firework
strong
radiant
shelter and sky
for a sparkler child

– Anonymous

INTRODUCTION

"It's probably best to wait a bit longer to send the letter."

I looked up at Brian across the kitchen table from me. The heartfelt five-page letter splayed out on the wood surface between us.

"What do you mean?" I said.

"Well," he said. He shifted in his seat and looked as though he was trying to find the right words. "Do we really know enough yet? What if we share something that we are really not sure we should be sharing or are even ready to share?"

"But," I said, also choosing my words carefully, "we agreed this was the right thing to do."

"I know," he said, "but honey, what happens if..."

"If *what*?" I said.

"What if we have to tell everyone later that we were wrong?"

I sat there, not really knowing how to respond to this. I understood his fear—to be wrong about this really could become a nightmare—but waiting, for me, would be agony all the same. It felt like I'd been holding onto this secret for forever, and I was ready to finally tell the truth. I'd always operated with the belief that secrets make you sick. *When I learn the truth about something, I should share it.*

"Brian," I finally said, "I feel like we're hiding behind something...a truth that I've honestly known about for a couple of years."

Brian didn't really say much in response to that, and I understood why things didn't seem clear to him. Given how society could be towards individuals who didn't fit easily into a proverbial 'box', this wasn't a revelation to share lightly. It's hard enough to share a truth that's close to the heart when it's about ourselves.

But what about when that truth is about our child?

Once I finally decided to write the letter, it was easy. I sat down one evening when Brian was putting the children to bed. I wrote:

> Dear friends and family,
>
> Brian and I want to give you an update on our beautiful Charlie. I write this with a heavy heart but also with strength I never knew I had. Sometimes life takes you down a path you never anticipated, only to show you that everything that came before was leading you to this very moment. And so goes our story.
>
> From the very beginning, we knew that Charlie was not a typical boy. He is so sweet-natured, so sensitive. When he was very young, he would actually stop and smell the flowers—which is funny now because our youngest, Oliver, will stop at a flower and proceed to rip it to shreds before moving on, (our children are polar opposites.) But we observed these behaviors before the arrival of Oliver. Charlie was always very drawn to women. We used to laugh and say, "What a ladies' man he is!"
>
> At two, he fell in love with Thomas and Friends, the kids' show about trains, but it was only the female engines he was really enamored with: Rosie, Caitlin, Belle, and his favorite, Emily. Charlie soon wanted us to call him "Emily" instead of "Charlie"—24/7. At the time, we thought it was cute (and a bit annoying) but we ignored any nagging feelings that something more significant was going on.

By three years old, Charlie's inclinations towards female identification grew even stronger. He started wearing a Santa hat and would run around telling us that the long top that folded over was his braid, imitating the ones so many of his favorite female characters had in books and on TV. It was almost impossible to get him to take it off. We thought maybe he just had a bit of an obsessive personality. It was unabating. I finally had to throw the hat away because Charlie had worn it so much that it was falling apart. Brian and I were actually grateful the day it went in the trash, even though Charlie was not.

Right around the same time as his braid obsession, Charlie was potty training. I'll never forget the moment Charlie ran into my room after a successful practice run with a stand-up pee session. I was so proud—until he started crying. Charlie ran into my arms, yelling through his tears: "I don't want a penis mommy, I'm a girl!"

My mind went in a million different directions. *He's just confused*, I thought. *He is too young to really know.* I had every thought you can imagine. It was as if that moment spread out for an eternity, but my heart knew at that moment what my mind was not willing to accept. I've heard women refer to this as their Mom Heart. In my Mom Heart, I knew who my baby was meant to be—but that doesn't mean I was ready to accept it right away. We all have our processes, our obstacles, and our fears.

At three and a half, Charlie told me, "Charlie ran away." He would cry and tell me that he "didn't want to be Charlie anymore!" My heart broke every time I heard him say these words. How could he not want to be my precious Charlie? How could he not like his name—a name that his father and I absolutely fell in love with when we chose it? Brian and I were confused. We were sad. We decided to reach out to a therapist that specialized in working with children who were gender-nonconforming, gender fluid, and transgender. We knew Charlie was special, different. We wanted to understand exactly what he was telling us.

We decided early on to let Charlie lead us instead of trying to control every situation—and this was hard for me, let me tell you! We allowed Charlie to take whatever steps were natural to him. One day, he wanted to wear a dress at home, and so we let him. Then, about a year ago, he corrected our pronoun usage. Charlie told us he wanted to use "she" and "her" rather than "he" and "him." We obliged. There were times when we thought it would fall away, that it was all only a phase, but Charlie's telling us he is really a girl was persistent and consistent over a long period of time. Over the past year, we have sought the expertise of professionals, read books, watched documentaries, and met with other families going through the same types of experiences with their children. We have had thousands of late-night talks, sleepless nights, and moments of weeping, but most importantly, we listened to our child.

Trust me, we really wished it was a phase, but Charlie kept moving forward, showing us and telling us that what we thought was the truth was not *her* truth.

A few months into preschool, Charlie told his classmates that his name was not Charlie, it was Elsa. Charlie had been completely obsessed with the Disney movie *Frozen*. While it may sound funny, Charlie truly identifies with the character of Elsa. Elsa is the person Charlie sees when she looks in the mirror at herself. To our relief, the preschool teachers were hardly surprised when Charlie asked to be called Elsa. They said they wanted Charlie—Elsa—to be happy, and they were supportive no matter what.

We have come to one solid, meaningful conclusion: although Elsa was physically born with male anatomy, her brain and heart is that of a girl.

Brian and I will be the first to admit that we struggle with it sometimes—not because we are ashamed of Elsa in any way but because it makes us worry for her safety now and later in life. There are so many bills on the desks of lawmakers that would prohibit our child from living her daily life in peace. It is beyond scary to think that our child may not be accepted for who she truly is and was meant to be. As the parents of a transgender child, Brian and I know there is only so much we can do to protect Elsa's self-esteem, but living in secrecy and shame is not good for any of us.

It is extremely important that Brian and I, as Elsa's parents, never shame her for expressing her true self. We will not be able to protect her from all the hateful and ignorant bullies throughout life – she will have to learn to navigate these obstacles on her own at some point—but we have been determined from the beginning not to let ourselves be our child's first bullies. By loving and accepting her unconditionally, we are instilling a confidence in her that will, hopefully, only grow from here.

We are respecting Elsa's persistent requests to live and present in appearance as a girl and to be referred to with she/her pronouns. We ask that you support our decision to let Elsa express herself freely, decide what to wear, and present to the world how she chooses. We all get this luxury. Why shouldn't she? We expect that you will love her, play with her, enjoy her company, and encourage her to be the happiest and best person she is capable of being.

These are the things we try to do to support Elsa and to help her build a strong character and sense of self. We hope that you, our family and friends, will help us. To that end, we ask you to:

1. Love her for who she is.

2. Validate her. Whenever it comes up in conversation, let Elsa know that you believe there is more than one way to be a boy or a girl and that you imagine it is hard that some kids don't get how you feel.

3. Encourage her individuality. Acknowledge and celebrate differences. She is different and knows it. When she wants to talk about it, talk about it; give examples of how you are different or how being different can be great!

4. Acknowledge your own prejudices. Recognize that some of your own individual issues about gender may play into your feelings about Elsa.

5. Be Elsa's advocate. If you are with her and in a situation where someone is teasing or judgmental, speak up for her and help her to speak up for herself.

6. Avoid victim blaming. Elsa is not responsible for other people's intolerance. She does not have to hide who she is in order to fit in. When people tease or bully her, they are the ones at fault—not Elsa.

7. Consider acceptance in other areas of your life. We all have to work on squashing eons of ingrained stereotypes. Examine the world around you and step up/speak out when someone is treated unfairly or unjustly because they are not like you and don't blend in.

We are sure this may be confusing for some of you. It certainly was for us at the beginning! What we have learned, however, is that most children realize their true gender between the ages of three and five. We have also learned that our child's transgender identity is not a result of our parenting style, family structure, or environmental factors. There is nothing anyone can do to change a child's gender identity. This is not just a phase for Elsa or something she will outgrow. Research has shown that therapeutic attempts to change a transgender child into accepting the child's born gender are both unsuccessful and detrimental to the child's mental health. So, understand that if you choose not to support our child's true gender identity, please don't expect our relationship to grow from here.

As parents, we want both of our children to be happy, feel good about themselves, and to find out what they are good at. These goals have not changed now that we recognize Elsa's gender identity.

We are aware of the uphill journey ahead for our daughter and for our entire family, but the alternative—denying who she is—puts her at high risk for depression, anxiety, acting out sexually, substance abuse, and suicide. Studies have shown that forty-one percent of transgender people whose families do not support their gender identities attempt suicide, at a rate twenty times the national average. We will not deny our daughter the support she needs. We hope you will not deny her your support either. Our family and friends are so important to us, and you will be important to Elsa as she goes through this transition. She needs to know that she is loved as a girl, just as she was as a boy.

I read something the other day about fear. F.E.A.R: Forget Everything And Rise. Rise to a new level of acceptance, understanding, tolerance, and love. We will do it together.

Love,

Tasha & Brian

I knew the revelation about my child might take some of our friends and family by surprise, especially those like my cousins that believed so devoutly in a religion that essentially taught them that anyone in the LGBTQ community was a sinner. I knew that it was such a new and uncharted discussion for so many people in our society, regardless of faith, and I also knew by now that no matter how hard we tried to explain our situation or how confidently we armed our child, she would still face a mountain of adversity in the years to come.

Among parents, I think there is a consensus that so many obstacles can stand in the way of their child becoming successful and loved. Children with disabilities face so much adversity. There are bullies now in every area of the country, in every school, ready to pick on others for anything that makes them different. It is a challenge these days for any child to feel like they belong somewhere.

If most children have a hard time fitting in and being accepted in this world for being who they are, I was terrified of what it might be like for my child. I was telling the world about her transitioning from male to female, from being born Charlie to becoming Elsa.

When Elsa fully transitioned to living as a girl one hundred percent of the time, I thought it would be a very difficult time for her. I thought she would be very emotional, confused, and angry, but again, I was making an incorrect assumption about my daughter. In fact, living as her authentic self was very easy for her.

In the end, this transformation period wasn't really about her transitioning into living as a girl. She always saw herself as a girl on the inside. She was so happy when it was finally complete. I realized then that I was actually the one who'd had a major transformation within myself. I had been holding myself back from truly understanding Elsa. My fear, denial, sadness, and confusion had kept me from fully accepting who she was.

This remarkable child was just patiently waiting for me—for all of us—to get on board with her, to know her fully and honestly. This is the story of how my daughter's life changed my own.

CHAPTER ONE

When Elsa started pre-K, I took her to orientation the first day. It was a great opportunity for her to meet the kids from her new class and for me to try to get to know the teachers and meet the parents of the new kids. A handful of kids had been in her previous preschool class, the one to which she transitioned mid-year. For those kids and parents, her gender identity was not a secret.

They understood her true gender identity and, from what I could tell, accepted it.

Everyone else, however, was new to our child. I kind of liked this scenario, for it was an opportunity to test people's acceptance levels for myself. While it gave me anxiety to think about anyone shaming my child for how they identified, I knew I couldn't hide behind these fears forever. I was proud of who she was.

I looked around the new classroom as Elsa got herself acquainted with some of the new kids. Not long after we arrived, one mother walked up to me and introduced herself.

"Hi," she began, giving me her hand to shake, "My name is Christina, and my daughter is Audrey."

"Nice to meet you," I said. "I'm Tasha and my daughter is Elsa."

"Oh wow," Christina started, "That's so cool her name is Elsa. She must have been over the moon when Frozen came out."

This was my chance to test her out. I was hoping she wouldn't let me down. While I was writhing inside with anxiety, I was also determined to face any opposition to my child head on.

I would take on the shame that might be directed towards my four-year-old, and I would squash it.

"Actually, she chose her own name," I said slowly, watching her expectantly. "She is transgender."

No going back now.

There was maybe a half-second pause, but then she said, "That's great. Very cool. It's wonderful you guys are so accepting of her."

It was precisely the response I had hoped for, but the truth was, even if she hadn't been immediately on board with it, I would have understood. Elsa was the first transgender person Brian and I had ever met. It was hard for us to wrap our brains around all the details at first, not to mention the discomfort and struggle associated with trying to understand how a four-year-old child just entering Pre-K can identify as transgender. Elsa's first day ended up going off without a hitch. For the parents and children that knew she had transitioned the previous year, the information was old news and treated as such. Nothing to see here, move along. The new kids and parents we met that day had no clue she was transgender—she presented as completely female. Her features had always been very delicate and feminine, her voice was like an angel's, and she was wearing a gorgeous purple flowered dress. She fit in perfectly with all the other girls in her class.

We made so many assumptions when we first realized who our child was. I assumed it wouldn't stick. She would change her mind. At first, I wished she would. For a time, I figured she was probably just a homosexual male and confused about this fact. I assumed it had to be experimental—no one this young could be so self-actualized. Making assumptions is the natural thing to do, especially in the face of the unknown. Yes, Brian and I were open-minded people who believed in equality for LGBTQ+ people—we had always supported gay marriage and had marched in Pride parades—but we couldn't really know how we would think, feel, or react until our own child put all of our beliefs to the test.

Elsa has given me—us—a gift of insight. Life may not be a picture-perfect fairy tale, but through her and who she is, I have been given the opportunity to access another aspect of myself.

I have been given access to a particular insight about life that, without her, I may never have encountered.

CHAPTER TWO

The boy was throwing an absolute fit.

He was being held by Rocky the instructor as he screamed, kicked, and cried uncontrollably on the surface of the pool's water. It was an indoor pool, specifically for swim lessons, and the noise reverberated off the cement walls at an insanely high decibel. I felt as if my ears were bleeding. Everyone was looking at our group, wondering whose child was having the tantrum. They looked incredulous as they stole glances at him, surprised at how intense his reaction was to the simple act of swimming.

Charlie seemed surprised as well. He sat on the first step down into the pool and stared at this other boy in his swim group as he threw his tantrum. Charlie's eyes were as big as saucers, and he gaped at the other child with a look that could only be described as horror. While Charlie waited patiently for his turn to swim with the instructor, the other boy continued to cry and kick his legs, looking like he was being drowned.

If Charlie had been the one throwing the fit, I would have fished him out of the water and high-tailed it out of there and never come back. I had such empathy for the mother of this boy because it was such an embarrassing situation.

Charlie, too, looked at the boy with confusion and almost disbelief. It seemed as though my child had a keen sense of what constituted decent public behavior, even though, at this point in his life, Charlie was only ten months old. From the moment he was born, Charlie was unflappable. His level of patience and calm demeanor always reassured us that we had an easy child on our hands. Before giving birth, I had worried about having an unruly boy to deal with, but that ended up not being the case at all. It seemed we had nothing to worry about with our boy.

Brian and I like to go out. It's not that we hate staying in; it's just that since we work in the food and beverage industry, going out to eat is part of what we do. We had prepared ourselves to not go out much (possibly not at all) after Charlie arrived, certain that the baby would throw a fit of some kind out in public, and we would have to leave an entire meal on the table of a nice restaurant, but it didn't play out that way at all. Charlie was so mellow—even in public—that we could venture out into the world with him. We even took our baby to many of the same places we did before we were parents, the non-kid type places, with white tablecloths and $15 cocktails. There weren't children's menus or highchairs anywhere to be found. It was like nothing about our going-out lifestyle had changed, except for the fact that I had a baby strapped to my front.

One night at an Italian restaurant, I was standing up holding Charlie while Brian ordered me a glass of wine at the bar. A frazzled-looking woman with two wild boys in tow gave me the once over and then turned back towards me quickly. She seemed to find it impossible not to speak to me.

"I can't believe how calm and well-behaved your boy is," she said. "I would expect this sweet nature more from a girl. I mean, that certainly wasn't my situation."

She then paused to glance over at her own sons. They were both standing on the booth benches, one with a fist full of food in his hand. I didn't know how to respond, other than to smile sheepishly and say thank you before she had to run over and practically tackle one of her children to the ground to stop them from fighting in the restaurant.

Before she headed out the door, she stopped by our table for one last comment.

"I hope you know how lucky you are. Boys just aren't like that. Enjoy it while it lasts!"

She said that last part with a wink, almost as if to say, "because it won't!"

It was almost uncomfortable, the amount of attention we received from anyone and everyone regarding our child's calm demeanor. Random strangers would comment, much like the woman in the restaurant, on how perfect our child was—especially for being male. Apparently, boys were supposed to be loud, unruly, and terribly behaved. We were constantly reminded of how blessed we were to have a boy like Charlie.

I had a nearly textbook thirty-seven week pregnancy, and he slept through the night at four months. He cried, of course, when most babies cry—when he was hungry, tired, or needed a diaper change, but the crying was usually short-lived and manageable, even out in public.

We, of course, knew that we were blessed no matter what kind of a baby he was, but all the attention paid to his temperament made me feel like I almost had to defend the fact that he was not a typically behaved boy. At the very least, I felt I had to offer some sort of explanation.

"He's very sweet and sensitive, isn't he?" I would say, almost like I felt that I had to defend his temperament. Sometimes I would just offer up how lucky we were before anyone could comment, leading with, "Charlie's not a typical boy at all. He's so calm and quiet. We got so lucky that we dodged the bullet and didn't get a rambunctious boy!" I would beat them to the punch so that I didn't have to hear the same comments over and over again. Besides, I already knew how lucky we were.

Another time, we were visiting with a couple of friends of ours who were parents to more aggressive, loud, and difficult boys. As we sat together in their living room, their boys were running around wreaking havoc. They kept pulling all the books off of the shelves and throwing their toys in the air. At one point a toy truck almost hit me in the head, and it was all I could muster not to go off on the red-headed three-year-old boy (whom in my head I had nicknamed "monster child"). My friend apologized to us for what felt like the hundredth time since we had arrived. All the while, Charlie just sat on the floor playing with blocks, not seeming to be affected by any of the chaos. The mother looked at Charlie and then shot us a look in turn. I could tell that she was embarrassed and slightly annoyed. Was she annoyed with her own children or annoyed with the fact that my kid was perfectly behaved? Maybe a little of both. Either way, the whole thing was awkward.

I often vacillated between wondering if friends and strangers were just jealous of our child's demeanor or judgmental of our family somehow, like being around us made them put a magnifying glass up to their own parenting style and challenged them to ask themselves hard questions. That wasn't our intent at all. Charlie was just being Charlie, and Brian and I were just winging it.

Brian and I were elated. He had been an easy pregnancy, an easy newborn, and an easy infant, and he was turning out to be easy as a toddler as well.

Our nanny, Margarita, took him to music class weekly, and even there he was well-behaved. He loved music. He would observe and really listen to the music being played. When he was ready, he would dance and sometimes try to sing along.

One time in particular, when I happened to sub in for Margarita and take Charlie to music class, I had an informative conversation with the teacher. Michelle, the college student who had been teaching the class for about six months, knew our child fairly well.

"Oh my gosh, you are his mom?!" she said. "It's so great to meet you. Charlie is so engaged in class. He listens attentively and is already trying to sing along with all the words. He is definitely not shy either."

She said this last part with a wink, and I already knew from Margarita that Charlie was quite comfortable approaching all the mommies in the room. The other little boys would typically run around the room and ultimately throw themselves—or each other—on the floor, which made Michelle's job even harder. Not Charlie. According to our nanny, he would either sit calmly in her lap and sing and clap along, or he would walk around the circle and find a mommy to sidle up to. She said he would sit there calmly and participate in the musical activities, all while staring up at the woman next to him. Everyone in the room got a kick out of it.

"Well, thanks," I said cautiously, "we are proud that he is already so polite...and engaging," I concluded with my own wink back at Michelle. I may have acted like I was surprised in response to Michelle, but I wasn't at all. At this point, Charlie's demeanor and behavior was expected—and gratifying—as a parent. I was thankful to have these kinds of conversations, as I knew many parents never did.

CHAPTER THREE

At age two, Charlie became obsessed with *Thomas the Tank Engine*. We only started letting him watch a bit of TV once he turned two, and Thomas was one of the shows he fell in love with right off the bat. He was so enamored that he took to memorizing as many of the engines as possible. By the time he was two and a half, he could name which ones were steam engines and which ones were diesel. (He couldn't comprehend what the difference was between the two, but he knew which were which.)

Right around the same time, Charlie entered another level in his capacity for language. Words poured out of his mouth more frequently each day. He told us all sorts of things that came to his attention. What he wanted to eat, what toys he wanted to play with, what shows he wanted to watch. The average boy at that age is able to say three-word sentences, but Charlie was able to say four- and five-word sentences. "Mommy, I want yogurt peez," he would ask for things so politely, already a rule-follower.

Sometimes I would playfully test his skills. One day, we purchased Charlie another Thomas the Train engine—Emily—at the toy store.

(He already had one Emily, but she was his favorite, so we caved and bought him another version of the female engine.) In the packaging for each toy train, I noticed that there was a flier with a picture of each of the Thomas the Train engines. I unfolded the paper and handed it to my son.

"Can you tell me the names of any of these trains?" I asked. I was interested in what was sinking in for him.

"James, Emily, Edward, Percy, Gordon, Mommy." He unflinchingly ticked off each of the trains on the first line of the paper. Granted, these were the most common trains on the Thomas the Train show, (besides Thomas himself) but I was impressed.

I leaned over and pointed at the pink engine.

"What is her name, Charlie?" I challenged him.

He looked at her for just a moment and then met me directly in the eyes.

"Pink is Rosie," he said with conviction.

Brian came down the stairs just after this exchange.

"Babe, Charlie can name many of the trains on this paper." I held the paper right up to his face, as if seeing it closer might make it a more profound statement.

Brian grabbed the paper, and his face lit up in a big smile. "Charlie! That's my boy! I'm not surprised. You are so smart," Brian exclaimed as he whisked Charlie up into his arms and spun him around.

My parents, and Charlie's only Grandma and Grandpa, finally moved out to San Diego in the months leading up to Charlie's second birthday and eventually took over caring for Charlie. While I know he missed spending every day with Margarita, he was overjoyed to have his Nana and Papa finally here on a full-time basis. They took nature walks with him and collected unique rocks, sticks, and the occasional feather, discussing each artifact with him as they went. Charlie listened with rapt attention, patiently looking for the next treasure as they spoke.

They loved to take him to restaurants, for he was always quiet and mild-mannered wherever they went.

This wasn't work, they said. This was a vacation.

Kids are typically expected to enter a difficult phase right about the time they turn two years old. We've nicknamed this time the "terrible twos" because children at this age are generally, well, terrible. But just as I'd grown to expect, Charlie didn't follow this customary timeline of childhood development. There never were terrible twos for our family, as Charlie met his toddler years with contentment, calm, and joy.

The words flowed out of Charlie like water around the two-and-a-half mark, and we noticed that he was also developing a proclivity for speaking to women. He would actively seek them out for a conversation anywhere—at the grocery store, museums, restaurants, the beach—wherever there were women around. If we met up with some kids for a playdate at the park, he would skip the part where he was supposed to play with the kids, and instead, he would sidle up next to one of the mommies and start talking.

The other boys in the playgroup threw sand in the air (and ultimately into other kids' eyes) or attempted to climb the play structure, but not our Charlie. He spent his time following around one beautiful woman after another, trying to talk to her for as long as she would listen. He didn't give up easily, and there was one time that was quite comical. After he lost interest rather quickly in the young children playing in the sand, he zeroed in on a tall woman with long curly black hair. She was sitting on a bench watching her son and daughter climb the play structure, and Charlie saw an opportunity to chat her up. I watched her engage him in toddler conversation—about Thomas the Train no doubt—all while keeping an eye on her own kids. After a bit, she stood up quickly and trotted over to her son, who was about to fall off the jungle gym. Charlie was fast on her heels, still talking. I had to muffle a laugh as I went over to pull my chatty child away. He came willingly but kept looking over his shoulder at the pretty lady as we walked back to our blanket in the grass.

When we went out to eat, we noticed that if a male was waiting on us, he could care less—it was almost like the guy was invisible, but if our waiter was a female, he would stare at her intently any time she came close to our table, and the feeling was mutual, as the waitresses always made a big deal over Charlie. He was so sweet that they couldn't help themselves from gushing all over him. (He ate it up too.)

Once when we took him for a quick bite at a cute neighborhood joint, he watched our waitress move from one side of the restaurant to the other and back again, all while eating his French fries.

I thought his head might whip around so fast he would hurt his neck. At one point during our meal, my eyes met Brian's, and I could tell he was thinking the same thing I was, boy, did we have a ladies' man on our hands!

A couple of weeks after we witnessed our ladies' man in the restaurant, I was getting ready to go to yoga and Charlie watched me get ready. I put on my yoga pants and tank top and then brushed my hair back into a ponytail. A flash of concern appeared across Charlie's face.

"Mommy, hair down."

"Charlie, Mommy has to wear her hair up for yoga. I can't wear it down; it will be in my eyes." I responded to him with logic, thinking that would work.

"No mommy, hair down. I want hair down," he said again, staring me straight in the eyes with conviction. It wasn't a request. I was expected to abide.

I had a strong feeling that he would not stop asking me to put my hair down until I did, so I decided to comply. I knew I could put my hair up once I arrived at my yoga class. For now, though, I could appease my son.

But this first instruction from Charlie to put my 'hair down' turned out to be the beginning of a pattern. He seemed to be obsessed with me always wearing my hair down. I could never put my hair in a ponytail or bun without him insisting that I put it back down again. At first, it was super cute, and I obliged. After some time, though, this obsession of his started to drive me crazy. It was *my* hair, for goodness sake! I could wear it however I wanted to!

And why did he care so much anyway?

But when I thought about it, I realized that while he was always drawn to women rather than men, he was most often drawn to the women with long hair, like me. Those women in the park or museums that he would follow unrelentingly usually had long, luscious hair. Blond, brunette, red, black—their hair color didn't matter to him, but the length did. My child seemed mesmerized by long, flowing locks. All I could think about was that my ladies' man preferred long-haired women.

It seemed to me that he had some kind of predisposition, an innate attraction to a certain type of woman.

Charlie also had an affinity for any female character in a show or story as well. He favored the female trains in the Thomas the Train series, with his obsession landing on the only girl that lived in the Tidmouth Shed with the boys each night: Emily. We bought him a toy version of Emily, and he took her everywhere with him 24/7. We couldn't pry the green engine out of his hot little hand no matter how much we tried. He was convinced that the black piping that framed the face of the engine was actually Emily's 'hair'. Everything female—real or imagined—had to have long hair. I had started to wonder, was this some weird fetish, or did my son wish to have long hair too?

Although Charlie continued to be obsessed with the Thomas the Train shows, we started to tire of them after months without a break. I was also slightly annoyed with his growing obsession with the Emily train in particular. I was annoyed because the train was female. Why wasn't he obsessed with Gordon? Or Henry? Or Thomas, for goodness sake? It was confusing. Out of curiosity, I wanted to introduce a different show to see which characters he would gravitate towards. I found a show called Super Why on PBS KIDS. The program centered on its characters solving a "super big problem," which they did by building reading skills such as learning the alphabet, spelling, and practicing vocabulary.

Each of the main characters were based upon characters developed previously for famous children's stories. Wonder Red is based upon Little Red Riding Hood, only this girl rollerblades and wears a slick hat rather than a hood; she is definitely a tough version of this character. Red has 'word power' and sings in rhymes.

Whyatt Beanstalk is the masked leader of the group and the younger brother of Jack from Jack and the Beanstalk. Whyatt has the 'power to read' and is able to fly into books to help solve problems and tell stories.

Then there is Alpha Pig, the tricycle-riding pig from The Three Little Pigs. He likes to pretend he is a construction worker like his dad, wearing overalls and a hard hat. Alpha Pig has 'alphabet power' and helps the viewers build words with him.

The last Super Reader to round out the group is Princess Pea. She's modeled after the Hans Christian Andersen story, The Princess and the Pea. She has 'spelling power' and twirls around in her frilly pink dress while flicking her wand to help children spell certain words.

Charlie devoured the first episode with wide eyes and laughed throughout. He was delighted, and so were we. After the show ended, he turned to me and, with a huge smile, said "Mommy, I'm Princess Pea."

I had imagined Charlie would identify with the main character, Whyatt, who was clearly a boy.

But instead, he chose to identify with the most feminine character there was. *Of course he wants to be Princess Pea*, I thought.

It made me wonder if I had a "super big problem" of my own. I couldn't figure out why my son wanted to identify with the most feminine character of the show—again. Did this signify something profound about my child? Again, I questioned why my son couldn't just be a regular rough-and-tumble boy who liked the stereotypical 'boy' toys. He was different, and I was afraid to acknowledge just how different he probably was.

Brian didn't seem all that concerned about Charlie's Princess Pea declaration. I, however, was beside myself with worry.

"Oh honey, it's just a phase," he reassured me one night after an entire weekend of referring to my son as Princess Pea. "He likes girl things. It's definitely different—nothing I've ever seen before with a little boy—but it will pass."

Maybe he was right. Maybe it would pass like so many children's phases do. Only time would tell. But in the meantime, it was a little awkward having to refer to my son as Princess Pea on the playground—were people looking at us? Did the other parents think my child was a girl? Did I need to offer an explanation? All these things went through my mind—thank god he wasn't in school yet! I was nervous to explain the situation to our friends as well. Our friends were wonderful, but I didn't want them to judge our parenting or our kid in general.

All kinds of worries bounced around my brain. Was Charlie gay? Could he even know something like that at two and a half years old anyway? That would explain his preference for girly things and characters, wouldn't it? I tried to push the thoughts out of my head, even as visions of drag queens haunted my dreams.

The obsession with Princess Pea endured for several weeks, and my anxiety went through the roof. I was so worried about what these tendencies meant for our child's future. I didn't have a problem with gay people at all—we have tons of gay friends. I really wouldn't care if my child were gay in the end. I just wanted to know what this behavior meant. Not knowing was killing me.

Brian, on the other hand, was still unfazed.

"Tash, it's nothing. He's just a different boy," he said matter-of-factly, trying to calm me down when I got all wrapped up in worrying again.

"We've always said that about Charlie. He has been 'different' from the time he was born. I know that, and for the most part, I love that about him, but this—this girly affinity, and especially this Princess Pea crap—well, it's just kind of weird, don't you think?" I was talking fast and biting my lip, my anxiety on full display.

"I know everything seems weird right now," he started cautiously, looking me in the eyes. "But this stuff makes him happy, right? And that's really all that matters right now. He will grow out of it, you will see. Try not to worry so much."

Though he said this, he also knows that it's pretty much impossible for me *not* to worry about most things.

He was right that Charlie was happy. He had always been a happy boy from the start. So what if the thing that was making him happy right now was pretending to be a character named Princess Pea?

We were at the top of the stairs, ready to walk down together, hand in hand, to get in the car. I was taking him to the Children's Museum for a few hours of fun on a Saturday—a much-needed break from the daily routine. I was feeling exhausted after a few weeks of referring to our son as Princess Pea, and I'd had several sleepless nights. Was it a phase? Or was this a sign of something I had yet to understand? Maybe he was just confused about gender? It seems like our society embraces tomboys, or girls who act more boyish and enjoy rough-and-tumble activities and sports. But our world is much less accommodating to boys that have 'girly' tendencies or interests. I needed more answers from Charlie about what he was really thinking and what he understood. I decided to quiz Charlie on the basics of gender.

"Daddy's a what, Charlie, boy or girl?" I asked.

"Boy, mommy," Charlie replied easily.

"Okay, what about Mommy then?"

"You a girl, Mommy," he said without hesitation.

"And Grandpa? What about him?" And Grandma?" I continued.

"Grandpa a boy, Grandma a girl." He didn't skip a beat.

"And you, Charlie? Are you a boy or a girl?" Now my heart was in my throat. I gripped the stair railing tight so as not to fall down the stairs—I could feel my knees already starting to wobble.

"A boy," he said quickly, and my anxiety began to lessen.

He looked into my eyes while he said it, but only for a split second. He then looked quickly away with what could only be described as thoughtful conviction. Before he could speak again, I rushed in.

"A boy! Yes, Charlie, you are a boy! Good job!"

I sensed something was coming next, but I felt that if I proclaimed his maleness out loud it would somehow supersede anything that came after.

"No! I'm a girl mommy!" He screamed, almost indignantly. Charlie was not a screamer. He was never loud. He never argued or threw a fit, ever. For him to raise his voice to me with such dramatic flair was alarming.

What was he saying? He was a girl? I couldn't even digest the information. I felt the pit that had formed in my stomach start to grow.

Charlie was a happy child, but with this declaration, I started to wonder just how happy he could be if he was this confused about who he was.

I looked into his eyes and said, "No, Charlie, actually you are a boy."

I thought I saw a flicker of sorrow flash across his facc. The look he gave me in return was one of confusion. He didn't respond.

We descended the stairs together in silence.

CHAPTER FOUR

In the summer of 2014, Charlie was two and a half years old, and I was in my third trimester with my second son, Oliver. I was ready for the pregnancy to be over. It was so much more difficult than my pregnancy with Charlie had been. Oliver kicked me in the tummy regularly, and I was constantly exhausted. I had developed gestational diabetes as well, a stark contrast to my nearly perfect pregnancy with Charlie. I had to check my blood sugar three times daily and eat snacks around the clock. Luckily, I was able to resign and take time to go through my difficult second pregnancy without the worry or stress of a job. I was thankful for the time off because, with the help of my parents, I was also raising a very active toddler.

One of the activities that I did regularly with Charlie was take him to the park. San Diego is such a great place to live because you can almost always enjoy being outside. Parks and beaches are an easy choice for kids' entertainment. Charlie was such a lover of nature that the park was an obvious choice for an outing.

There was a large playground and tons of restaurants in the area. I wanted to let Charlie play for a while on the playground and then we could finish the day with some good food (I wanted to eat all the time).

We got to the playground in the late morning, and it was full of children, parents, grandparents, and nannies. I found a bench to rest my exhausted body and watched Charlie run off to a group of kids playing in the sand. Just before he reached the group, he deviated and took a turn towards a couple of ladies talking on the perimeter of the playground. *Oh lord, what is he up to now*, I thought as I watched him begin to engage the women with his toddler conversation. One of the women waved goodbye and walked away from the other. That left one woman, with long blonde hair, standing next to my son. She was watching her two towheaded children run rampant on the playground but remained thoughtfully attuned to Charlie all the while. When she moved to another part of the play area, Charlie readily followed her, jabbering away. I could see the woman's face change a bit. I could tell she was beginning to get annoyed with my son's chatter. I carefully lifted my huge self from the park bench and headed in Charlie's direction. The woman shot me a quick look of relief when she realized that I was the chatty child's mother.

"Charlie, let's leave this lady alone and find some kids to play with," I said, coaxing him over to me and grabbing his hand. "Okay mommy," Charlie responded, still watching the woman with the long blonde hair as he approached the group of kids in the sand nearby. But he did not engage with the children in the group like I thought he would. After about ten minutes of silently scooping sand into a bucket, he jumped up and trotted back over to the woman.

"Oh my god," I said to myself under my breath. "I don't have the energy for this."

I awkwardly waddled back over to retrieve my child for the second time. I was a bit embarrassed—I didn't need complete strangers to think that Charlie was some weird kid. Weird kids are picked on in school—judged, ostracized from activities and targeted by groups in society. I wanted my kids to fit in and belong—to be accepted.

But his repetitive behavior was just that—weird.

Not only was Charlie's obsessive nature with women in public an embarrassing concern, his liking for all things feminine was also picking up speed. He had taken to having us call him by female names. If my friend Lauren came over to visit, he would insist that we refer to him by the name Lauren for the rest of the day. He was still obsessed with the Princess Pea character, which was also a favorite nickname for himself. For me, it got weirder by the day. As if I didn't have other things to worry about in the last three months of my pregnancy!

Things were so confusing—and somewhat frustrating—with Charlie's behaviors that I couldn't focus solely on the pregnancy.

There were instances when I felt like he behaved like a regular little boy—like the time he held a twenty-foot python at the Del Mar fairground—and for a moment I would stop worrying so much.

We went to a children's fair one weekend for something different to do. There were booths set up for kids to win contests, sign up for zoo passes, or for parents to gather information regarding schooling choices. On one end of the building, there were a few small animals in cages that the kids could look at and even pet. We made our way through the crowd over to the guinea pigs and bunnies. As we approached, we noticed a booth housing a very large and very yellow snake. Anyone who dared could sit on a bench next to this huge, slithering beast and take a picture. (There was no way I was going to do something like that. I hated snakes! They gave me the heebie-jeebies.)

"Mommy! A snake! I want to pet the snake!" Charlie declared passionately.

He almost squealed with excitement when he saw the creature.

I paused for a second, letting it sink in that my son wanted to do something that was stereotypically very 'boy' in nature.

At first, I was shocked. Then I was elated.

"Oh, of course, Charlie! You should! I'll get a picture of you and Daddy," I volunteered quickly. I wanted to take advantage of this moment to really foster what I saw as a masculine interest. Charlie sidled right up to the twenty-foot python without an ounce of fear. I took dozens of pictures of Charlie and that snake. I wanted to make sure that this moment was fully captured.

I was so proud of my little boy.

I would have these fleeting moments of calm when it came to Charlie's behavior, but most of the time I didn't feel this way. Most of the time, I was anxiety-ridden and deeply confused by the things Charlie said and did. If the constant need to be referred to with a female name wasn't enough, the echo of his (more frequent) declarations that he was, in fact, really a girl rang in my ears and clouded my mind.

It got to the point where I was stressed out all the time. Between the difficulty of my pregnancy and deciphering Charlie's whims, I was stressed out all the time. I needed answers but didn't know where to turn.

Did this behavior have to do with his sexuality or identity? Was it a phase? Was there even a name for what he was experiencing? The whole thing was driving me crazy. I had to have some answers.

I turned to the one source that I thought could help ease my distress: Google. I took to obsessively Googling any phrase that related to what I thought might be happening to my son. "My son thinks he's a girl," was one of the sentences I typed in the Google browser. "My boy likes girl things," was another search. Then, "Is my son gay?" This one was a stretch because my son was only two and a half, and I doubted he had any idea yet how he felt sexually, but at this point, nothing could be completely ruled out.

My Google searches opened up a treasure trove of information. Some of it was insightful and helpful, and some of it overwhelming—and sort of scary, but I was able to read stories written by moms who'd had some of the same experiences as I had with Charlie. One search led me to an open forum where people could post their questions about their kids and others could chime in with their opinions or advice. It seemed like a good place to bounce concerns off other parents, to make sure I wasn't alone in my plight. I wasn't yet ready to post anything, as I was still pretty private with the things I had observed. I simply wanted to read other people's experiences.

Some moms' testimonials (and a few dads') were heartwarming to read. One woman wrote a very consoling paragraph to another mom, reassuring her that her son or daughter would grow out of the gender-bending behaviors that they were displaying. It had been just a phase for her child, she wrote.

Whew. That made me feel better.

Just as I read that, I scrolled down to another account from a mom whose experience with her son was almost exactly like ours with Charlie. I scrolled down further to see if another parent had responded to her post. One person offered a response suggesting that the child in question was most likely "gender fluid." She went on to write about her own experiences and how, after years of speculation, her child ended up identifying as gender fluid.

I had never heard this term before: gender-fluid. It sounded like a trendy drink or a genre of dance, not an identity descriptor. I googled "gender-fluid" next. I came across this definition on Wikipedia:

"A person who is gender fluid prefers to remain flexible about their gender identity rather than committing to a single gender. They may fluctuate between genders or express multiple genders at the same time."

The Urban Dictionary site described it this way: "Gender Fluid is a gender identity best described as a dynamic mix of boy and girl. A person who is gender fluid may always feel like a mix of the two traditional genders, but may feel more boy some days, and more girl other days. Being gender fluid has nothing to do with which set of genitalia one has, nor their sexual orientation."

This gender fluid thing sounded a lot like Charlie. Sometimes he was distinctly boy—like with his love of Thomas the Train and the brave snake encounter. Other times he was much more feminine—his Princess Pea declaration and long hair obsession came to mind. Could this gender fluid term fully describe my son? I had a friend once tell me her brother liked to wear his mom's high heels around the house and even put on her makeup from time to time. Flash forward twenty years and he's a fully-grown man now, married to a woman with two kids. It had been just a phase for him. What was the likelihood that it was just a phase for Charlie as well?

After everything I had read, I had a sinking feeling in my gut. I was consumed with dread for what I thought was happening. Charlie had such a sense of conviction when he asked us to refer to him as Princess Pea. He didn't seem to be simply playing. He wanted us to take him seriously as not just this character, but as a girl. If I knew anything about Charlie, I knew there was a soulfulness about him. He was a serious kid and nothing was kept on the surface. I knew there was something profound happening in his little head; I just didn't know what.

Ordinarily, whenever I researched anything medical, I referenced only reputable medical websites for answers. Regular people's opinions were of no interest to me, for I felt there was no certifiable validity to them. When it came to parenting Charlie, however, I was willing to read other parents' opinions and experiences. When I read some of the comments posted by mothers regarding their child's confusing gender identity, I knew that I was not alone.

I needed to find out what Brian thought of my initial research. He was always bringing me in off the ledge whenever I spun a bit out of control. He was calm in my gale-force windstorm. He would be sure to tell me if I was on to something or just imagining things. I approached him one night after Charlie was in bed, and we were settling in for the night to watch some TV.

"Honey, I would like to talk to you about some things I've researched lately," I began. He muted the TV and turned towards me to listen.

"Okay," he said, a bit tentatively. "Is this about Charlie by chance?"

"Yes, it is. I googled a bunch of topics related to little boys who pretend to be little girls. There's a lot," I continued nervously, looking down at my hands. I rushed on with the information.

"There are so many moms that have almost the exact same experiences with their little boys. One mom said she is pretty sure her five-year-old son is gender fluid."

I had never said the term "gender fluid" out loud before, and I looked Brian straight in the eye when I did. I paused to let him ruminate over the terminology I had just presented.

"Gender fluid? You mean someone thinks they're one gender one day and the other gender another day? That kind of a thing?"

His questions were rhetorical.

"I understand that there may be people out there who are defined this way," he said, "but how can you possibly think that it defines our Charlie? I mean, he is not even three years old. Don't you think that is super early to assume anything? Especially about his identity or sexuality?"

He was a little less calm than usual, a bit defensive.

"Well it says that sexuality and gender identity are completely different things," I jumped in.

"Okay, well, great. Even if they are, how can we know about a child that isn't even three yet? How could he even know? They don't even diagnose children for autism until they are at least three! Like I already said, let's not jump to conclusions. I feel like this is still some kind of a phase. Please try not to worry so much. You get yourself so worked up and this is something that we have to wait to play out. I know that's hard for you, but you have to try."

He said this with a finality that let me know that I needed to drop the subject for now.

But I wasn't going to drop it, at least not altogether. I could not sit around and wait for things to play out. That, to me, would have been like waiting in some type of purgatory.

I decided to talk to my mom. She was my other voice of reason.

My dad had a Master's in Psychology, but for some reason, I was less embarrassed to talk to my mom about my obsessive googling habits.

One afternoon when my dad was at the store, I cut right to the chase. "Mom, do you think kids can have fluidity in their gender? Or that they can identify as the opposite gender of their birth? How do you think that happens?"

I fired off the questions quickly, and at first, my mom appeared taken aback. She took a moment to reflect on the questions.

"Oh honey, I know you are thinking a lot about Charlie. It is confusing, I agree. But let's not jump to conclusions. He isn't even three yet," she said. She paused. She could tell I didn't love this answer, so she offered another insight.

"You know, I remember questioning the origin of gender following some discussion in my Early Childhood classes in college—way back in the late 1960s. So then when I worked at my Head Start center after I graduated, I encountered this four-year-old boy. He was playing in the dress-up area, and as he sat down beside me in his pretty pink dress, he looked up at me in a solemn way and stated that he was a girl. In that moment, I had no doubts that he was." She paused, thinking about her delivery of the next part of the story.

"His outside didn't match how he felt inside. It was like his brain told him what gender he was, regardless of what his private parts—or society—said he should be. That was the first time I had met someone that seemed to just know that about themselves. Even at such a young age, I just believed that he knew."

She looked me directly in the eyes and continued, "True gender identity must be in the mind."

In the mind. Gender identity must be in the mind.

After hearing it, I couldn't get the concept out of *my* mind. It seemed so right.

But my mom broke into my thoughts again. "I just wonder what happened to that child. I hope his family at least tried to understand him. Society wasn't as accepting of LGBTQ people back then," I could see the worry flooding her face as she spoke. "With the harsh stigma of being different, I wonder if that child was able to live authentically as a girl," she paused to look at me carefully before she continued. "Or if they survived…at all." She looked down, her eyes filling with tears.

Suicide. That's what she had meant. Good god. I knew she was right to consider this, especially in the 1970s, but I couldn't bear to think that that was what could have happened to the child she had known.

Because gender is in the mind, I thought to myself again.

I tried very hard to keep my hands from shaking as I typed into the Google search bar: "Rates of suicide for LGBTQ youth." What I read was astounding. LGBTQ youth are almost five times as likely to have attempted suicide compared to heterosexual youth, according to The Trevor Project, an organization that provides information and support to LGBTQ youth 24/7, all year round. Close to forty percent of transgender people have attempted suicide at some point. Then I read that transgender people who are rejected by their families or lack social support are much more likely to both consider suicide and to attempt it. What gave me hope, however, was that those with strong support were eighty-two percent less likely to attempt suicide than those without.

It was all so depressing and scary. I was terrified that Charlie somehow fell onto the spectrum of fluid-gender identity or sexuality. I knew deep in my heart that I would love him no matter where the story led him—where it led us. What I was afraid of was whether or not my love would be enough to protect him—from ridicule, heartache, bullying, loneliness.

I lay awake at night, going over every little thing he said or did that might be perceived as feminine in nature. *How many times today did he declare he was Princess Pea? Was he staring at that other mommy because he thought she was pretty, or does he wish he was actually her?*

If there was a day when the female inclinations abated, I would get very excited and hopeful. I would pray that he had turned some sort of figurative corner. In the rare moments that Charlie seemed to be comfortable—dare I say even joyful—in his maleness, I had the fleeting thought that maybe all the confusion would just go away. But those moments came and went, and all the gender identity confusion came roaring back.

One particular morning after I'd had a restless night of anxiety and worry about my son, I came downstairs to find him sitting on the couch watching TV. He was wearing a knit stocking hat that had the face of a frog on the front. This should have been funny to anyone who caught a glimpse of him, not just because the frog face was comical but because he was wearing a knit hat during an Indian summer in San Diego. It should have been hilarious.

But instead, my heart sank. It wasn't the hat, which was super cute, but rather what the hat represented. On the bottom of the hat, on either side, were long braids. I guess a person could tie them under their chin to keep the hat on or just wear them as they were for a laugh, but previously, my son had requested that we tie the braids in a ponytail behind his head. I knew he wanted to emulate having long hair. Reluctantly, not wanting to upset him, I gave him a ponytail. I watched him admire himself in the mirror once it was on his head, moving his face from side to side to see how the ponytail moved back and forth. He was elated with the look. I decided to just let it go—he was happy after all. It was all the other incidents that had led to this that were upsetting me, and well, I guess I also understood that this wasn't going away any time soon.

It was, after all, the fifth day in a row that he had worn the hat.

I went back to Googling. This time I wanted more specific answers regarding what was happening to my boy. I googled the usual "female tendencies in little boys" but came up with mostly the same information I had encountered before.

I took a deep breath and typed in something else.

"Is my child transgender?"

All kinds of posts came up then. There were a few mommy blogs and a couple of articles from reputable newspaper publications.

And then I saw a video on YouTube. It looked vague enough at first. It was entitled "The Whittington Family Ryland's Story". Intrigued, I clicked on the link and the video began with the beautiful music of Jeff Buckley singing Leonard Cohen's "Hallelujah". The video went on to introduce a baby girl named Ryland. Her family discovered at a year old that she was deaf. They found a way to help her to hear—cochlear implants in her ears. They thought their struggles were over. Now that she could hear, she could also speak for the first time. Once she could speak, she started screaming to them that she was really a boy.

In a poignant scene in the family's bathtub, Ryland and her younger sister were happily playing in the water. Ryland looked into the camera and announced, "I'm a brother," the child exclaimed, out from under a head full of golden curls. She looked like a girl, but she clearly did not feel that way about herself. The tears rolled down my cheeks as I thought of my own child's declaration on the stairs that day. *"No mommy, I'm a girl!"*

The scene cut away to a sentence on the screen.

"Although Ryland was born with female anatomy, her brain identifies with that of a boy."

A knife cut into my heart. Her brain identifies with that of a boy. "True gender identity must be in the mind," my mom had said. I sobbed as I thought about what all of this really meant—about Charlie, our family, his future. A wail caught in my throat a couple of times as I watched the rest of the seven-minute video. I realized that Ryland's story was our own—my son's. For the first time in six months, everything made sense.

I was not the mother of a boy, but rather a girl. Charlie had been a girl all along.

I had a transgender child.

CHAPTER FIVE

When I was first pregnant with Charlie, I asked Brian if he wanted to find out the gender of our baby before the birth. Some of our friends had kept it a secret till the very end and would often say "it's the last real surprise you have in life!"

"Well, I know that some people like to wait for the surprise, but I don't know; what's the harm in knowing? Preparing?" Brian responded to my question about gender exactly as I thought he would. He was a planner like me. More often than not, we both preferred to not be surprised. I mulled it over for a total of five minutes. I was the impatient one. "I agree, honey. I mean, how would I decorate the baby's room if we didn't know what color theme to focus on?" I replied, as if this was the most pressing issue of the pregnancy timeline.

Though we wanted to find out the gender as soon as possible—around 18 weeks—we just both figured and hoped our baby would be a girl. At the ultrasound appointment, the radiologist put a warm clear jelly on my belly while Brian lovingly held my hand. He was all set to be a doting dad; I could already tell.

The radiologist moved the probe around on my belly. This was the moment I had waited my whole life for.

"And…" the radiologist said, "Your baby is… a BOY!"

She looked up with excitement.

I looked back at her. I was obviously supposed to mirror the excitement she had offered with the news.

But I couldn't.

I thought in my gut that the baby would for sure be a girl. I looked up at Brian and thought I saw a flicker of disappointment in his eyes as well, but then he spoke.

"Oh, that's so great!" he said.

"Oh, wonderful," I said, looking away.

But my head was swimming with anxiety, disappointment, and a bit of fear. I had always pictured myself being a mom of a girl. I wanted to get pedicures and put on makeup together. I dreamed of helping her pick out her prom dress and eventually her wedding dress. I was ready to tell my daughter all about what to expect in puberty, prepared to eventually have a talk about sex and birth control with her. What was I going to do with a boy? I knew nothing about boys. I didn't have brothers. I had a great father and, of course, a wonderful husband, but other than that, my feelings toward men in general were still a bit dismal. I had been a self-described feminist since I could remember. Historically, women had been held down by men in societies all over the world. I wouldn't go as far as to say that I thought that males were inferior to females, but I suppose I had a bit of a chip on my shoulder towards the opposite gender. I had also been so hurt by the young boys who had bullied me in adolescence. Even though I now had great examples of men in my life, I worried about raising one. I felt as though it would be so much work to raise a boy to be a responsible, kind hearted, loving man. Society provided pressures for boys and men that I was nervous I was unequipped to deal with. Boys these days need to be sensitive and loving, but also strong and resilient. It was akin to balancing on a tightrope. I was terrified of raising a boy who would be one of those bullies I had encountered, and worse, turn out to be a total jerk of a man. I'd never forgive myself. With a girl, I just had to protect her, teach her to be strong and tenacious like me. I figured I could do that.

But now, it was thrust upon me. I had no choice.

I would have to do my best.

Once the news sunk in, I took on the information with gusto and charged full steam ahead. That was how I had handled most uncertainties in my life up to that point. I jumped into decorating the baby's room, picking out my favorite shade of blue to paint the room, and buying bedding with cute lambies printed on it. After all, as Brian had reassured me on our ride home, the most important information we had gleaned from the ultrasound was that our baby was perfectly healthy. The rest we would figure out as we went.

I grew up in a very small town in Southeast Nebraska. It was 600 people small.

I knew early on in my life that my small town was too small for me. Almost everyone who lived there was white, middle-class, Christian, and straight (or so we thought). I could tell at a very young age that this was not an accurate representation of the people in our country as a whole. The lack of diversity was stifling.

But even though we lived in our own sort of homogenous bubble in small-town Nebraska, my parents always had a pretty progressive view of life. They were always striving to venture outside the proverbial box to learn, be challenged, and in turn, grow as people.

My parents had grown up in small towns in Nebraska themselves. They met at Chadron State College in western Nebraska during the late '60s. They were both influenced and affected by the struggles of our country at that time. My mom's first year was 1968—the same year that Robert Kennedy and Martin Luther King, Jr. were murdered. The Vietnam War raged on, and the draft was in full force. But before 1971, according to the Selective Service System of the US Government, a young man could qualify for a student deferment if he could show he was a full-time student making satisfactory progress in virtually any field of study. These men could continue to go to school and be deferred from service until they were too old to be drafted. As a result, people from all different places and backgrounds were attending their small Nebraska college. Dodging the draft wasn't the reason my dad enrolled in college. He always knew he would go, and he could easily run track at Chadron. His draft number was high enough anyway, so he wasn't too worried about going overseas regardless.

At the same time, the women's movement was in full swing. My mom's love of and talent for writing secured her a job at the school's newspaper. She wrote about the inequities facing women, in society and particularly at their small college. My mom was eager to bring about change where she could, and she started with the archaic rules at Chadron. She, with the help of a few of her sorority sisters, got the college to agree to allow women to begin wearing pants to class.

At a young age, I longed to meet people who were different from me, as my parents had. I grew to believe that I didn't belong in this small farm town in Nebraska.

Growing up, I knew I saw the world differently than many of my classmates. I sensed that there was so much more to the world than what the small-town life of Nebraska could offer. I knew everyone wasn't the same race, religion, or had the same culture—though we had little evidence to support these facts in our little farm town. Instead of trying to fit into the same mold of all the kids in my school, I wanted to be able to embrace my differences and celebrate them, even if the differences weren't that apparent on the surface. But differences were not celebrated in my small school of 100 students. For instance, if I dressed differently than other kids (basically this meant wearing something other than a t-shirt and jeans), I was teased mercilessly.

"Wow, look at Tasha's parachute pants! What in the heck? Is she gonna jump out of an airplane later? Ha ha!" I could hear the snickering as I walked to my locker in my new MC Hammer pants. It took every ounce of strength I had not to conform to the other student's idea of what kind of wardrobe was deemed acceptable. I remember wishing that I could just express myself with my clothes, but also with my ideas. I was very opinionated and outspoken. I started to butt heads with other students beginning in junior high—namely a group of brutish boys in my class.

A boy named Danny was the ringleader. Several childish boys in my class mimicked his rude behaviors and laughed at every joke he cracked. It was so annoying because it was always at the expense of others. I was often on the receiving end of his insulting "jokes". He was more than uncouth—he was downright mean—and no one stood up to him. One day I'd had enough. "Did you see Mrs. Richards' dress today? It looked like she was wearing a tablecloth!" Danny laughed, looking to his buddies for validation. Ken and Tim piled on immediately with their own insults.

"Can you imagine what size her underwear is?"

"Oh my god, as big as a house!" Raucous laughter erupted from the group.

I rolled my eyes. "Why don't you guys shut up? You are such a bunch of immature jerks!" I snapped.

The laughter halted instantly. Danny turned toward me with a scowl. "Oh really? And what are you? Your nose looks like a beak and you're ugly! Shut up yourself."

Even though I thought Danny was a jerk, his words cut like a knife. I didn't know how to ignore their immaturity, and I also didn't have the patience to wait for them to grow out of their bad behavior. The endless teasing and name-calling took a toll on me, but I was too stubborn to learn how to keep my mouth shut instead of calling them out.

It became a vicious cycle, and I continued to be bullied by them throughout high school. It often felt like torture. I developed very aggravated feelings towards boys. I was angry at them for bullying me, but mostly, I was very sad that I wasn't accepted by them either. That was the weird thing. I didn't really like any of those mean boys, but for some reason, I still wanted them to like me. I wanted nothing more than to be fully accepted and ultimately respected for who I was and all my differences.

Brian's growing-up experience was so much different from my own. He was from a larger family—he was the youngest of four siblings—in the much larger city of Phoenix, Arizona. While I grew up to question Christianity early on, Brian was taught the opposite growing up in a deeply religious household. Early on his family was Catholic, but ultimately became Pentecostal when his mother decided she wanted to become a minister. Growing up, his faith was central in his life, and the Bible was never questioned in their home. They went to church as a family every Sunday. His respect for his parents, especially for his mother, was paramount.

Brian is a larger man now, standing at six foot four, but he was a little guy for quite a long time. His nickname was "Little Elk" throughout most of elementary school and even into high school. He didn't have a big growth spurt until he was about nineteen. Despite his small stature, his red hair and freckled face, he was never bullied by his peers and always stood up for any kids who were. He has said that he was always pretty confident and almost always felt accepted by the kids in his school.

Not only was it at a later age for Brian to grow physically, he was a self-professed "late bloomer" when it came to his innocence too. For him, the world was pretty black and white, and he didn't question much of what he experienced. If he encountered anyone in the LGBTQ community growing up, he either didn't realize it at the time or if he did, just figured it was a lifestyle choice that he didn't understand. He actually had a few family members who identified as gay, and one was sent by the church to a type of conversion camp for a time. It didn't work, of course, and the boy came back still as gay as he was when he left for camp. (Thankfully his family loved the boy all the same).

From the time we met, I was aware of Brian's upbringing in a very Christian household. I had seen his views become more progressive through our conversations over time, and I felt we were on the same page regarding many topics.

Brian and I had been dating for several months when I decided it was time for him to meet my parents. I'm an only child, so my parents' approval is very important to me, especially with regard to a man I thought I would marry. I was meeting my mom and dad in San Francisco for the week and invited Brian to fly up and join us toward the end of the trip. I hadn't had many boyfriends in the past, so I needed some time to tell them all about my new beau before he met up with us.

He arrived in a taxi just as we were coming out of City Lights bookstore, and we made our way across the alley to the pub. It was dark and cool in the bar, and we had to wait several seconds for our eyes to adjust so that we could see our way to a table in the back. It wasn't until we sat down that we realized every wall in the place was covered in pictures of male genitalia. Some were drawings, others were graphic photographs. Here I sat between my future husband and my parents, completely surrounded by penises.

I did not come from a very modest family, but this was enough to make all of us uncomfortable! It was hilarious and shocking at the same time! My dad was the first to break the silence.

"I went to college with that guy," he pointed at one of the black and white photos of a rather well-endowed man on the wall behind my mom's head. He managed to keep a straight face for a few seconds as we all looked around the table at each other awkwardly. Knowing this couldn't possibly be true but was instead just another one of my dad's crude attempts at humor, I burst out laughing. Everyone else joined in, and the tension in the room immediately diminished. At least for a bit.

The minute our drinks were plunked down in front of us, my mom launched in. "So, Brian, I hear you're a Republican," she said, matter-of-factly. The tension was ratcheted up a notch.

"Uh, oh, well," Brian stammered.

I could tell he was uncomfortable with the question, caught off guard by her directness and feeling somewhat vulnerable in the presence of all the male nudity.

"I did vote for Bush, but I wouldn't consider myself a Republican," he said, pulling it together. "I try to vote on the issues, not the party."

I swallowed hard. I knew it was a strike for my mom that he had voted for Bush, but he had finished strong. I waited for her reaction. She slowly took a sip of her dirty martini.

"That's good," she replied. "You grew up in a conservative family, right?" I decided to intercede the conversation and help him out a bit.

"Mom, Brian is from an Evangelical family, but he is not conservative in all of his views," I tried to reassure them.

Brian started again, this time more confidently. "Joyce, I did grow up in a more conservative family in Arizona; that's true, but I can tell you, since living in California for the last twenty years, I've definitely grown to have more liberal views regarding many social situations."

Good answer, I thought to myself. I looked carefully to my mom, trying to interpret the look on her face.

"Wonderful to hear, Brian," she said as she smiled at him warmly.

I breathed a sigh of relief.

We were married the following year.

There were times when I was still taken aback by his belief system and the assumptions about certain groups of people that that mindset had helped him to create. I remember when we were first married, and my mom and dad came for a visit. My mom, Brian, and I were up late one night engaging in deep conversation about everything from climate change to Obama's presidency, to the Civil Rights Movement. The subject veered off into a discussion about gay marriage. "Oh, my goodness, I really hope that the Supreme Court can ultimately legalize gay marriage in this country. It is way overdue," my mom slammed down her glass of wine on the coffee table to emphasize her passionate opinion. I grabbed a napkin to quickly wipe up the red wine that had sloshed out of the glass before it stained my white faux marble table.

"I agree mom. Why is this still being debated? Homosexuality has been around since the beginning of time. They were born that way, after all. It's not like their sexuality is a choice. Why can't they just marry whomever they love?" I was extremely passionate about the topic myself, as I had several gay friends at my current job at the wine bar.

I looked over at Brian, who hadn't chimed in yet on this topic. He was looking down into his wine glass. I wasn't sure if he was just lost in thought or if he had noticed a fly swimming in his Merlot. He looked up suddenly with a serious look on his face. "You think they were born that way? I mean, I wonder, is it not a lifestyle choice?" It was a question, but it sounded more rhetorical to me. My mom jumped right in before I could open my mouth.

"What? A choice? You're kidding, right?" She didn't wait for him to respond before she continued. "How can it be a choice? Why would anyone *choose* a life path that is not fully accepted in society, one that is even denied some legal rights too?" She set her wine glass down more carefully this time but shook her head firmly to show her disapproval of Brian's comment.

Instead of coming to Brian's defense, I backed my mom up. "Yeah, Brian, look, that's just not true. I mean, the lifestyle thing. I remember this Psychology of Sex class I took senior year of college. The professor talked about parts of the brain that were the same size for those of gay men and heterosexual women. There's something to that," I paused to take a breath, "And I had a co-worker a couple of years ago that told me he knew he liked boys when he was five. It was just a feeling that was innately there." Brian's eyes were wide, like we had surprised him with all our conviction.

"Oh, okay. Wow. Well, I just don't know," He was being careful not to set us off. I knew he had a lifetime of conservative conditioning with his religion. It was precluding him from accepting the information my mom and I were giving him. I felt completely defeated when I went to bed that night. How could my husband not agree with me on this topic? Was he more closed-minded than I had thought? I tossed and turned until morning, thinking of how to convince him I was right.

In the end, I didn't have to convince him at all. The very next morning, Brian walked up to me while I was doing dishes and kissed me on the cheek. "Morning love," he started off slow, unsure of what my mood would be after a night of intense conversation. I rebuffed him a bit—I was still upset—so he launched right in, wanting to smooth things over. "So, I stayed up late last night. I was doing some research," he paused to gauge my body language. I had stopped washing dishes and turned to face him. "I was researching homosexuality. If people are born that way or if it is a lifestyle choice," I waited for him to continue. I hoped he had come to the right conclusion.

"Basically, you were right. I was wrong. Everything I read supported what you and mom were telling me. There is homosexuality in a lot of the animal kingdom. It must be biological." I scanned his face for sarcasm, but there wasn't any. He was being serious. I was shocked. Although he had spent over forty years with one way of thinking, he took the time to research and then educate himself on the opposite way of thinking. On top of that, he was able to admit he had been wrong. I was blown away. I had been wrong too. He was more open-minded than I had realized.

I approached Brian about getting pregnant after we had only been married six months. We both knew we wanted kids, but until that moment, I hadn't told him I was actually ready to do it. It was like a switch had flipped in me, and now was the time.

I knew there was a possibility that Brian and I would have a hard time conceiving. My mom had suffered several miscarriages and almost ended up adopting. It's the reason I am an only child. They always wanted more than one child, but over time they had to accept that they were only meant to have one. I decided to look at our future pregnancy in the same way. Whatever was meant to be, would be. We would manage.

Then we conceived our child.

There was no "trying," no tears, no sleepless nights, and no languishing hope. Just like that, we were pregnant.

We couldn't believe how lucky we were.

CHAPTER SIX

I had a visceral reaction to seeing the YouTube video of the trans boy, Ryland Wittington. I didn't know if it was what people called "mother's intuition" or something like that, but I just knew that there was a good chance my child was transgender too. What else could explain all of his odd behaviors and actions, from his obsession with female characters and long hair to his declarations that he was, in fact, really a girl? I had, after all, always been taught by my parents to ask questions. I could remember questioning the Bible—and religion in general—at around nine years old.

My very religious cousins had come to visit us in Nebraska, and it wasn't long before we were debating Biblical stories in my bedroom. Sitting cross-legged on my Strawberry Shortcake bedspread, I responded with conviction to my cousin Amy's declarations of Noah's Ark.

"Do you think they could have put polar bears on that boat? Or kangaroos? How would they have gotten them all the way from Australia?" The story just didn't make sense to me, logically or geographically. My cousins didn't really have answers to my questions, other than since it was in the Bible it was most definitely true. If that's what God wanted, then God made it happen.

Is that what had happened with my child? God had made my child transgender? Why? Why would a God of any kind make a child live a harder life? I just couldn't believe it. I had decided in the last few years that life was just random, and *science* was very complex.

Brian was not on board with the idea that our child was transgender. Unlike me, he had been raised to think of life as black and white. There was an explanation for everything, and often God was involved in that version.

He witnessed what a wreck I had become while watching the video about Ryland. He tried to comfort me through my tears, while also attempting to halt my ever-increasing paranoia regarding my child's identity. One evening in particular, he tried to comfort me as I was in the middle of a particularly intense episode of crying over this issue.

"Oh, honey, you are so upset," he started as he put his arms around me in that big bear hug of his. He hadn't watched the video in its entirety but had seen enough to know why I was so emotional.

"That was some video," he continued. "An amazing story. But, love, I feel like you are going down the rabbit hole of worry—jumping to conclusions too quickly," he continued, though tentatively, as not to further upset me.

"Babe," I exclaimed through my sobs, "I just have a feeling in my heart-gut-whatever that Charlie is transgender! It all makes sense now!"

"Transgender? Honey, come on. This is such a new term to be throwing around. We hardly know what that means. I agree that our Charlie is different—that he's a bit confused about what he likes and maybe who he is. But to think that he is a *girl trapped in a boy's body*? He's not even three yet! It just seems crazy to me. I know this video resonated with you, but we can't just assume that the situation is the same for our child. He is not a 'typical boy', and he is confused about some things, but that is all we know—all we *can* know—for now."

He said this with finality in his tone. Once again, I knew I was not going to convince him of all my heart's forgone conclusions—not now anyway. Brian's reaction forced me to really think about what was going on in my heart and head.

Maybe I was jumping the gun with my assumptions of Charlie's behaviors. It could be a phase that would work itself out as he approached his third or even fourth year. He could be homosexual and just not know anything about sexuality yet. These behaviors could be like a precursor for what was to come down the line later when he realized his first crushes.

Or, despite my intuition otherwise, he could just be an odd kid.

Period.

Brian wanted to take everything in stride and see how it all developed. That was going to take time and the kind of patience that was hard for me given how I remained ever wary. But time did go by, and I grew less absolute in my feelings. Of course, that might have been in part because I was about to give birth to Oliver at any moment.

With all the kicking and punching Oliver was doing inside my belly, it seemed as if he was just as ready to come out as I was to be done being pregnant. But then, he had beat me up constantly since the day I felt his first movement. Charlie had moved gently through my belly, almost as if he was doing a choreographed water ballet routine. It was light, gradual, and almost tender. The whole pregnancy had been blissful, and I worked until the week before I delivered. With Oliver, it was quite the opposite. I'd be watching TV in the evening with Brian and almost jump off the couch when he kicked or punched me swiftly in the side. I'd let out a high-pitched yelp at the same time, startling Brian.

However, he quickly got used to the nightly activities in my belly, courtesy of our second child. As I got bigger, we could see the little hand or foot imprints pushing out on the sides of my belly each night. It was like an alien was stuck inside, trying to push its way out.

And, as I would soon learn, this was just the way that he would approach most things in life. Oliver went gangbusters right from the start. At least I'd had a warning.

Life with two kids was more work than I had anticipated. Charlie was such a well-behaved and good-natured child, but even still, just trying to meet the needs of two small people every day took its toll.

While Charlie had not cried much as a newborn, this couldn't have been a starker contrast to Oliver's beginning. Charlie had also loved being swaddled (wrapped up like a burrito) to sleep at night. When we would go to get him in the morning, he was most often still in his perfect swaddle. Oliver, on the other hand, usually punched or kicked his way out of the swaddle before the first morning light. Brian took great pride in being an "expert" swaddler (I could never get it tight enough) and was always dismayed when Oliver was still able to escape even one hand from the almost suffocating wrap he had concocted. This kid was nothing if not strong and tenacious.

Brian swears to this day that Oliver was so strong that he even lifted his head off his shoulder while he was holding him at only six weeks old, even though most kids can't do this until they are around four months. So I wasn't even sure this was possible, but either way, it seemed as though Oliver was a strong one.

Oliver was also more of a crier. His newborn photos were no exception. It was a delicate dance to get him to pose for more than one picture before his little face would crumple and tears would start to rain down. With the newborn photos, we wanted to get a few shots of the baby alone. We had plenty of Mama and baby and Daddy and baby. Every time I tried to lay Oliver down solo, he wailed and wailed. He did not want to be without Mama! Charlie was a big help during the photo shoot. Luckily Oliver was okay with Charlie next to him for comfort on a couple of shots. We laid them on our bed together with Charlie's arm around the baby and it nearly took my breath away—the cuteness of them together! Charlie played the part of big brother well, alternately calming his baby brother and then taking his own moment to pose for a charismatic shot.

I could already see that my sons were so distinctly different from each other. Sometimes it was shocking—even frustrating—but it was also fun to see two individual personalities forming before our eyes. When I found out I was having two boys, I had assumed that I'd have two very similar children. This was not going to be the case at all. We appeared to have two polar-opposite little boys.

There had always been a certain amount of uncertainty swirling around Charlie's short little life. While we were elated that he was such an easy-going child, I, at least, was always waiting for some unknown thing that was about to happen. What would we discover about him next? What would he say that would throw us for a loop?

And the question that always seemed to plague my mind—was this all just a phase?

Oliver's first few months offered a bit of reprieve from the worry over Charlie's behavior. I simply didn't have as much time to ponder what all the ambiguity regarding Charlie's personality really meant. What Oliver's presence in our lives demonstrated right away was significant. He was unequivocally 100% boy. He was loud and he seemed to have a bit of a temper. Oliver's demeanor seemed to match the stereotype of what a male was. It was Charlie that gave me so much uncertainty. All those friends—and strangers—that commented on how atypical Charlie was started out as flattering, but then it quickly became very annoying. Why couldn't a boy be sweet-natured, quiet, well-behaved—even as an infant or toddler?

Also, why couldn't a boy like girl things? After all, girls liked typical "boy things" all the time. Girls played in the dirt, wore pants, and these days some even played football. These kinds of girls were referred to as "tom boys" and were generally accepted for not being as outwardly feminine as other girls. But boys who liked girl things? Well, they were known far more pejoratively as "girly boys." It was supposedly abnormal for a boy to present feminine traits or to have what was perceived to be feminine interests. These boys were usually categorized by others as homosexual (even if they were, in fact, heterosexual) and often shunned because of it. There had always been a double standard when it came to gender-associated traits and interests. At least that seemed to still be true for how people viewed and categorized the gender of children.

Adult men, on the other hand, are finally able to present other more atypical attributes than in the past. I've watched countless TV shows over the last few years that really highlight a man's stereotypical "feminine" side—Queer Eye for the Straight Guy, Top Chef, all the interior design shows on HGTV. These activities aren't just for women anymore. It just goes to show that women of today often want a man who is "well-rounded" or in touch with his feminine side, so to speak. Men who can cook and do laundry are embraced positively. Men more routinely participate in childcare duties, often with as much frequency as moms do. I like to call these men "Renaissance Men". They can—in essence—do it all. They can cook, clean, and care for children, all while changing the oil in the car and fixing the light bulbs around the house. It was nice to know men could be stereotypically "manly" while also not being afraid to tap into the sweeter, softer side of themselves.

So what if that was it? What if my Charlie was a Renaissance man in the making? Brian was, after all. He was surely born with more of a softer demeanor and a sweet-natured soul—he likes musicals for goodness sake—but it didn't happen overnight. The trait was perfected over time. Though Brian was my very own Renaissance man with a cherished feminine side, he was still distinctly male.

When I had gotten over the initial shock of having a baby boy, I grew quite comfortable with the idea. I had always subscribed to a particular cliche regarding boys versus girls: Girls were *more* difficult as they grew older, and boys grew *less* difficult with age. I was okay with not having to worry about a teenage daughter talking back, sneaking out, dating! If I could get through the crazy toddler years with boys, the rest would be a breeze! Ironically though, having boys was turning out to be anything but easy.

I couldn't answer all the questions I still had surrounding Charlie's behavior, but I could relish in the conviction that I had with Oliver. While he drove me bonkers with the crying, throwing of toys, and the pure magnitude of his strength and presence, I knew for sure I had a boy as stereotypical as it appeared to be. For once, I welcomed the stereotype.

Charlie's presence was large in our lives but filled the spaces not taken by every other member of our family. His calmness and quiet nature slipped into the cracks in the crazy moments when our lives needed to be more tranquil and soft. His presence made us reflect, appreciate, and ponder. For this, I was truly thankful.

CHAPTER SEVEN

I have always loved Halloween. The costumes, the elaborate decorations, and of course all the candy received from trick or treating! I was bound and determined to have my children love Halloween just as much as I did for as long as possible.

In the lead-up to the big day, I bought a few Halloween-themed books to read to Charlie, hoping to get him in the proper Halloween spirit. I was excited to find one at the bookstore that was new to me but appeared to capture the holiday theme exceptionally well. It even had a sing-songy cadence to it—perfect for an almost three-year-old.

The book was called *Room on the Broom*. The main character was a witch with long orange hair and a big nose, complete with a wart at the end of it. The witch was a total sweetheart. She joyfully, yet clumsily, flew about the forest with her grumpy orange cat on the back of her broom. Along the way, she dropped things—first her hat, then her cloak, then her hair bow. Each time she flew down to the ground to retrieve her lost item, she discovered an animal waiting to give it back to her. She encountered a dog, a bird, and a frog. Every one of them wanted to know if there was "room on the broom" for them to ride too. Since the witch was so sweet, she always said yes (much to the cat's chagrin). I couldn't wait to read this story to Charlie.

One night, at the beginning of October, Charlie sat in rapt attention as soon as I began to read to him. As I turned each page, his eyes grew wider and wider while he listened intently to the story.

When I closed the book after reading it the first time, Charlie screamed with unabashed enthusiasm, "Mommy, again! Read it again!"

So I did.

After the second time through, I suggested that we move on to another of the Halloween books I had purchased.

"No, Mommy! I want *Room on the Broom* again!"

I read it three more times, and it ended up that *Room on the Broom was* the only book I read to him that first night. Even though I was a bit tired of the *Room on the Broom* story, I was extremely pleased that Charlie loved it so much. I was quite confident that my child would love Halloween as much as I did.

We set about finding the perfect Halloween costume for Charlie. He was finally old enough to really enjoy trick-or-treating, and I wanted him to have the cutest costume on the street. I googled "kid Halloween costumes" and was flooded with all kinds of ideas. I imagined Charlie as a raccoon or a fox. I considered a pirate or a firefighter—but he had years to be either of those. I had to find the one that was just right.

My mom nearly had a heart attack when I mentioned the cost of the costumes I had found online over dinner at our house one night.

"Oh that is ridiculous!" she said. "You don't have to pay $100 for a costume he will likely wear one time. That is just crazy."

She had a good point, but I was willing to shell out some dough for Charlie to be the cutest kid in town.

"You know," my mom continued, "we never bought a costume for you when you were a kid. I always made you one."

She looked me in the eyes, almost as a challenge.

"*Every* costume mom?" I said. "Really? Okay then, why don't you make one for Charlie? But it has to be pretty creative!"

I had put the ball back in her court. Now she had to help me. Just as she was preparing to tell me that she would gladly make the cutest costume for her grandson, Brian spoke up.

"I'll help you make Charlie a costume. We can do it together. I think it could be really fun," he said.

He looked from me to my mom, wondering if he had softened the slight tension between her and me. Mom didn't miss a beat with her response.

"Brian, that sounds great! I would love to! What were you thinking we could make for him? Any ideas?"

Brian spoke quickly, as if he had been thinking about making Charlie a costume for weeks.

"Well, I was thinking maybe something with Thomas the Train. He loves Thomas," he paused for just a second and then rapidly continued speaking his thoughts out loud. "I think we could make a train costume for Charlie, one that he could wear."

"Yes, I like that. Could we find a box that he could wear around his body? There would need to be a hole for his head and his arms," she excitedly offered.

"Yes," Brian said, fired up about the idea. "It will be like he is actually the engineer inside the train driving it. I love it!"

My mom had already started sketching the costume on a blank piece of paper. I watched them pour over the plans together. I was already confident that Charlie would have the cutest *homemade* costume for Halloween this year—and as an added bonus, I had saved 100 bucks.

When I first introduced *Room on the Broom* to Charlie, I thought it was the most adorable Halloween-themed book I had ever read.

It quickly became the most annoying book I had ever read.

Each night Charlie would race over to his bookshelf after bath time and snatch *Room on the Broom* from the pile on top, his eyes alight with excitement. "Mommy, I want *Room on the Broom*! Read this!" He would thrust it immediately in my face before I had time to find an alternative, let alone breathe. He acted as if we had never read it before. But we had read it before. We read it every single night and sometimes more than once.

"Okay, Honey. Are you sure? What about *The Giving Tree*? Or *Go Dog Go!*?" I tried to coax him towards something—anything—besides *Room on the Broom*. He had so many books!

But no. He had become obsessed with the story and demanded that I read it every night. When your child loves something so much, especially a book, you say "yes" when they ask you to read it to them again.

Then one morning I came downstairs to find Charlie running back and forth across the living room with my kitchen broom between his legs.

"Mommy, I'm a witch!" His eyes were wide with exuberance as he raced in circles around the furniture.

I had to admit to myself that this scene was super cute. It was until he came to me thirty minutes later with Oliver's baby blanket in his hands, "Mommy, can you help me?"

I wasn't sure what he was referring to at first. He placed the blanket over his head and looked up at me with those beautiful brown eyes. I then realized that he wanted me to help him attach the blanket to his head to make it look like long hair, just like he had done with the frog hat and the braids.

He wanted to become the witch in the story. It was fortunate that he was emulating such a sweet little character, but I was confused once again by Charlie's behavior. Why was it *always* a girl character rather than a boy? I knelt next to him and tied the baby blanket like a head scarf under his chin. He grinned up at me with gratitude before he quickly ran off to get his broom. I had a sneaking suspicion that *Room on the Broom* was going to be around long after Halloween was over.

We set out on Halloween night without an ounce of trepidation. Charlie was dressed in his handmade Thomas the Train costume, and Oliver was snuggly in his stroller. We were ready for a fun night. We set out for our trick-or-treating that night in a neighborhood of San Diego where the residents spent a lot of time (and money) on their elaborate decorations. We couldn't wait to see what they had cooked up this year.

We spent an hour or so walking up and down the wide, beautifully-manicured sidewalks of Mission Hills. We saw houses covered in spider webs and others were engulfed in fog and smoke. Some of the homes we walked by were noisy; we could hear blood-curdling screams and sinister laughter wafting out from the windows and doors. It was all for fun, but so much of it was very realistic! I was a bit worried about Charlie becoming completely terrified. He was only just about to turn three, after all.

He seemed to be fine with all the scary machinations that we encountered until we approached a mechanical witch. We turned a corner, and there she was in all of her creepiness, at least two feet taller than Charlie. Not only did she move her arms and head back and forth every few seconds, she also spoke. The witch warned: "I'll get you my pretty! AWHHHHH HAA HAA HAA!" *Predictable,* I thought, but those words could haunt a kid's dreams at night!

Most children walking by the house stayed far away from her. No one Charlie's age dared to get close. I thought for sure that Charlie would freak out and cover his eyes or at least walk quickly past her like the other kids did.

Instead, he walked right up to her and stared. Mouth gaping open, he stood there mesmerized.

"Mommy, she's talking to me," he said, not taking his eyes off the figure as he stood there in his innocent little Thomas the Train costume. "She's real, mommy," he said.

He wasn't scared of her at all. He wanted her to be real. I was amazed. After about ten minutes of staring at the witch, I finally got him to move on to the next house, but he would not let the witch go.

"Mommy, can we go back to the witch house?" he asked me at least twenty times afterwards, as we walked from house to house. I eventually gave in, and we circled back to the house for one last glimpse of her. He remained transfixed for the rest of the night, obsessing over the witch until bedtime.

I wondered why.

After the mechanical witch experience on Halloween, Charlie's witch obsession became even more amplified. Charlie was flying around the house on his broom again, Oliver's blanket perched awkwardly on his head as he went from room to room. As I saw him, I thought, "Let me guess, now you are Room on the Broom?"

"Mommy! I'm Room on the Broom!" He exclaimed. I had to admit it was funny, even cute. The witch in the story was never given a name, so Charlie referred to her simply as "Room on the Broom." Then he became Room on the Broom himself.

He wouldn't let us call him by any other name. If we slipped up and said, "Hey Charlie," he would quickly correct us: "I'm Room on the Broom, Mommy."

I couldn't get used to it. I had named my child Charlie. I didn't want to call him by some other name. It was frustrating and, frankly, very silly. Months earlier, I thought Princess Pea was a weird character for Charlie to emulate, but at least she had a name.

I hoped that if we played along for a while and called our son Room on the Broom, he would eventually get bored of it and move on to something less ridiculous. Maybe if we appeased him in this situation, he would put some of the other obsessions to rest? It was worth a try.

"Room on the Broom! Would you like strawberries or grapes for snack?" I'd call from the kitchen to where my son was watching TV in the living room. "Strawberries, Mommy!" He would holler back quickly. I rolled my eyes as I opened the refrigerator to grab the fruit he wanted. I did my best not to let Charlie see my frustration over the odd name change.

"Here you go Room on the Broom," I said as I handed my son the bowl. There was an unmistakable look of gratitude in his eyes as he turned towards me to grab the bowl.

Then, as I was about to return to the kitchen, I saw something else flash across his angelic little face.

Pride.

I understood that kids often like to role-play. Pretending helps children understand the world and their place in it. It was natural for a kid to pretend to be a doctor, a fireman, or a teacher. I would often see kids dressed as various superheroes on the playground. I had talked to moms that said that their child had been dressing up as Batman almost every day for a week. They were frustrated with it and didn't see it ending any time soon.

But these situations were so different from ours with Charlie. It wasn't just that we also couldn't see him letting up any time soon with his pretending to be a character. It was the character he chose to portray that was hard to swallow. We were so perplexed with why he had chosen to emulate a female character rather than a male one. The way I had chosen to dress in school had made me a target for teasing by my classmates. The last thing I wanted for my child was to stick out like a sore thumb and become a target himself. At this point, I would have given anything for him to be parading around in a Batman, Spider-Man, even Darth Vader costume for weeks on end. It would have been annoying, but at least I would have felt like my child was behaving like a 'normal' little boy. I just wanted him to fly under the radar, to not be so different from other kids that it would be harder for him to fit in. I tried to convince myself that Charlie's differences from other kids simply made him more interesting. I know every parent thinks their child is special, but there had always been something unique, exceptional, distinctive about Charlie from the very beginning.

After several weeks of incessantly referring to our son as "Room on the Broom," I was going nuts. Not only was I still very confused by his behavior, I was now beginning to miss Charlie. It was like there was an imposter living in our house. He was still my child, of course, but he very clearly didn't want to present himself as Charlie, a little boy. He seemed so much more comfortable pretending to be a female witch. I kept asking myself if I would feel the same way if I came home to a child version of Batman every night rather than an unnamed witch character from a children's book. I wasn't quite sure. All I knew for sure was that this had to stop, or I was going to lose it.

I snuck into Charlie's room before bedtime, while he was still engrossed in a TV show downstairs. I scoured the shelves for *Room on the Broom*. I found it lodged between a Dr. Seuss book and *Goodnight, Goodnight Construction Site*. I snatched it out quickly and tip-toed swiftly over to my son's closet. Above his three built-in dresser drawers, there were several shelves reaching all the way to the ceiling. All of the shelves were too tall for Charlie to ever reach, and he would never even think of doing so anyway. I had filled the shelves with extra towels and sheets, nothing of interest to him.

I had to think fast. I knew Charlie could come looking for me at any time—I could hardly ever go to the bathroom without being followed. I lifted one of the folded towels and promptly slipped the thin paperback book in between it and another one folded underneath. Perfect. *Room on the Broom* was effectively out of our lives, at least in the book form. My hope was that if we stopped reading the book to Charlie each night, he would eventually forget about it, and my real son would return. We couldn't read it if we didn't know where it was, right? I just had to figure out what to tell Charlie.

As I thought about what to say to Charlie about the book, I heard him behind me. "Mommy? Daddy said bedtime."

"Oh, uh, um, yes, Honey. Let's get in the bath," I stammered, a bit flustered by his sudden appearance and the encroaching guilt I was starting to feel.

After bath time, while getting dressed for bed, Charlie asked me excitedly, "Mommy, read *Room on the Broom*!" But tonight would be different.

"Honey," I looked him in the eyes, gathering as much courage as I could, "*Room on the Broom* went away."

His eyes widened in concern, and he said, "Why mommy? Where did the book go?"

"Oh, honey, we are just going to read other books for a while. We've read that one many, many times."

I tried to soften the blow with a small smile of reassurance. He glanced around the room slowly with these huge puppy dog eyes, his mouth slightly turned down like he was going to cry at any minute. I think he hoped it would turn up suddenly and this horrible game I was playing would be all over with. Reluctantly, he picked another book to read. It was like I had broken his heart.

I hated myself for making him feel this way. I never wanted to hurt my children, ever. Truthfully, though, I was at a loss regarding how to handle Charlie's obsession, and I had acted on impulse. I hoped my feelings of shame and guilt would subside once Charlie started to forget about the book.

Just as Charlie was about to turn three, we decided to tackle potty training. Oliver was about a month old, and I finally had enough energy to devote some time to getting my firstborn out of diapers. I also didn't want to have two kids in diapers for any longer than I had to.

I was not prepared for what Charlie screamed from the bathroom a couple days into the training.

"Mommy, I don't want a penis!"

I was in my bedroom down the hall, as I had just left him standing over the potty to get used to doing the training independently. But when I heard his words, I froze. Panic rushed over me. Charlie then ran into my room viscerally upset, tears streaming down his face. I bent down on one knee and pulled him close to me.

"It's okay, honey. Everything will be okay," I said to him, not even convinced myself.

I had no idea what else to say.

This was the first time he had expressed disdain for his male anatomy. I knew there was an extra focus on his parts now that he was working on standing over the potty. I held him and ruminated over our options. If I wanted him to potty train now, I didn't have many options to speak of except one.

"Sweetie, why don't you try to sit down on the potty to go pee pee?" I asked him gently, looking into his red-rimmed eyes. He nodded, seemingly satisfied at least for the moment that he didn't have to be reminded of his anatomy every time he had to go to the bathroom.

Inside though, I was conflicted. I had so many questions swimming in my head. Was I condoning this anti-male behavior of his? Plenty of grown men peed sitting down, didn't they? Lots of little boys sat down to pee when they were learning—it didn't mean anything, did it? In a way, this was a quick fix for Charlie. I couldn't bear to see him so upset. I was still avoiding the bigger questions, like what was really going on with him, and what was I going to do once I found out?

Christmas presented us with a new set of confusing challenges. What kind of presents were we supposed to get our son? He was still into Thomas the Train but had also started to venture towards more genderbending toys. I had broken down a couple of months prior and bought him a Princess Pea doll. He carried it everywhere like it was glued to his hand. I justified this purchase because he was still actively playing with male-oriented toys, such as cars, trains, and blocks. I told myself that kids really shouldn't be raised with the idea that they should only play with gender-specific toys.

After all, it was society that forced these gender "norms" on kids, right? Charlie recently asked to carry a purse like Mommy and would be ecstatic to get one for Christmas. I mulled over that option, and I settled on finding a bag that was nondescript. It didn't have to be pink or purple; it could be a more neutral blue or green. I remembered that Joey had a "man bag" on Friends once, and he was still macho.

All these thoughts were still racing through my brain while we put up our Christmas tree on a warm San Diego Sunday in December. I was in a zone and hadn't noticed Charlie at first when he bounded over to me as I hung the tinsel on a branch. When he spoke, I was jolted back to reality.

"Mommy, look at my long hair!" he cried with a huge grin spread across his face.

He had found a red Santa hat amongst our holiday decorations and had it happily perched atop his head. Because the top of the hat was very long, it flopped over and fell down to the middle of his back. Of course, he was pretending that this hat was his hair. *Here we go again,* I thought. We'd been down this road before. I knew I'd be looking at that Santa hat on his head for the next three weeks until Christmas. Every day. All day.

I was so sick of the sight of that hat that the day after Christmas I took it (not off his head, I waited until bedtime!) and threw it in the trash. Charlie had worn the thing out, and it was falling apart, so I was justified in my actions. And Christmas was over! At this point, I wondered if it would just be easier (and less weird) to just let him grow his hair out. I hadn't let him grow it before. I hadn't wanted Charlie to look any more like a girl in public. I was trying to control what I could. I still wanted this to all be a phase. But at this point, long hair would be so much easier to deal with than a baby blanket or an old Christmas hat on his head! After all, Brad Pitt looked pretty great with long locks in

Legends of the Fall. Hell, Brian even had a ponytail back in the nineties. Both were very manly.

It had been a long year. One spent mostly in a fog of confusion. I hoped that the New Year would bring us some clarity where Charlie was concerned. I had spent so much time, especially in the past couple of months, bargaining with myself. "If I do this or say this, then Charlie will react this way or that," or "if I take this away, his behavior will change or stop." I had made so many concessions with my son. I had bought him a couple dolls and even a purse for Christmas. I had acquiesced and referred to him as Room on the Broom for weeks on end. I was exhausted. Nothing seemed to go the way I thought—or hoped—it would.

I knew when I decided to have children that it would often be challenging, yet still rewarding, but there was no handbook for the kind of things we were experiencing with Charlie. I had so many questions for which I could not find answers.

I had reached my breaking point.

CHAPTER EIGHT

At three and a half years old, Charlie's verbal declarations of his gender identity were only getting more frequent. Any hope that this behavior would taper off as he grew older sunk down deeper into the pit of my stomach. By now, Charlie wasn't just pretending to be female characters or telling us that he was a girl —he was starting to do something else.

One night, Brian and I were in the kitchen before dinnertime.

"Honey," I said, thinking we were alone. "What do you think he wants for dinner?"

Charlie quickly jumped out from where he was hiding in the dining room.

"*She,* Mommy," he shouted, "not *he*. I'm Emily." He had a look of frustration in his big brown eyes.

Emily was a new identity, derived from his favorite Thomas the Train engine—the only female to have a spot at the famed Tidmouth Shed.

She.

We had to change our pronoun usage? What was next?

I gritted my teeth, forcing back the urge to correct him and say, "No, you are a he."

I couldn't say that. Nothing would change his behavior.

Instead, I said, "Oh, I mean *she*. Sorry, Emily." It was like choking down my mother's stroganoff when I was younger—I had to pretend to like it.

With that one reassurance from me, Charlie bounded off into the living room to watch Thomas the Train with a sly smile on his lips. I must have had a sad look on my face when I turned to Brian. He could sense that it was my turn for reassurance, and he moved in closer to me to put his arm around my shoulders.

"Honey, he's being Emily now. She's his favorite train. It's okay. He's still watching Thomas and playing with trains, isn't he?" He swung his head covertly towards the living room to check on Charlie's proximity. "I mean, *she*."

He said that last part lovingly, as he turned back, though it was almost to poke fun at me and my neurotic tendencies. I had the inability at times to "go with the flow," and this was one of those times.

"Okay, honey. I'll chill out," I said in return.

But as the words tumbled out of my mouth, I knew that would be practically impossible for me to do.

A distraction from my worries about Charlie came in the form of a new job. After eighteen months of unemployment, most of which I spent pregnant with Oliver, I was ready and willing to go back to the workforce. I loved my kids, but I also could not be a stay-at-home mom. I would lose my mind. Being unemployed had given me bonding time with Oliver especially, but it had also robbed me of my identity.

Unemployment had also given me too much time to sit and ruminate over Charlie's current behavior and possible future.

I loved my new job in wine sales. I was using my experience and knowledge from years in the restaurant industry while still learning new things. I also had a varied schedule, bouncing from store to restaurant and back several times a day. I still had a schedule, but my position also allowed for flexibility. I didn't have to punch a clock. If I had to take one of the kids to the doctor, I could. The job kept me on my toes and provided a necessary diversion from what I perceived to be family drama.

But on occasion, I found unexpected downtimes throughout the day. An appointment would cancel at the last minute or a buyer would be running horribly behind, and I'd be forced to wait. In these moments, my mind wandered. Sometimes I would start texting my parents. Since they were the children's daycare providers, they bore witness to everything Charlie said and did.

I wanted to know which character he was portraying on any given day. Had he referred to himself as a girl at all? And most concerning to me, had he corrected my parents with their pronoun usage?

My parents were always reassuring, and at times I believe they downplayed my child's behavior so as not to alarm me.

"Charlie has been playing trains all day. He only told us to call him Emily twice."

Once I texted them three times in a day, paranoid. "He's been wrestling and tickling with Grandpa for the last half an hour. I see a bit of a rough-and-tumble boy coming through. Don't worry," my mother said.

My parents' responses to my obsessive texts would dictate much of my mood each day. I was so grateful they were there for me and my child. I believed that if I was privy to every single moment of my child's day, I could find a span of time in which he was just a boy being a boy.

Right? That was something I needed to hold onto. But after a couple months, my daily neurotic texts prompted my mom to have a different kind of response.

"How many times has he insisted he is a girl today?" I texted her. "And how exactly did he say it when he did?"

I could see the little dots forming on the screen, a sign that my mother was typing. The dots disappeared a couple times and then reappeared, which only made me more anxious awaiting her response. Finally, her words showed up on my phone: "Honey, you must stop doing this. You must let us live our lives and take this day by day. Somehow you need to try to stop controlling this and just let it be."

The words seemed to pulsate on the screen as I read them repeatedly. My mom had totally called me out. She didn't shy away from speaking her mind, but I wasn't expecting this response. It dawned on me at that moment how obsessed I had become with my child's identity. My parents were telling me that they'd had enough.

I knew I had to find peace of mind elsewhere.

One day later that summer, I was getting ready for a special girlfriends' spa day for my birthday celebration and making sure that everything was taken care of before I could go and relax. I confirmed that Brian knew what foods to feed Charlie and that he knew the location of the new formula container for Oliver in the cabinet. I packed in a hurry.

I was so focused on everything I had to do that I almost missed Charlie moping about the house, following me from room to room. On this day, he had an aura of sadness about him. His overwhelming sorrow was palpable. Something was bothering him.

I got down on the floor to play with him, and he immediately wrapped his arms around me in a huge bear hug. Mama bears know when their cubs need extra love, so I just held him for a few minutes. When I finally pulled back, I said, "I love you, Charlie."

His eyes looked forlorn, searching my face for comfort, acceptance.

"Charlie ran away, Mama, and he's not coming back!"

I felt like I was going to throw up. My son had reached a whole new level. I was so shocked that I didn't even know how to respond. I needed a moment to recover, get my bearings.

"Honey, what do you mean?"

It was all I could muster. I was feeling desperate now. Charlie didn't mean this. He couldn't.

"Charlie ran away!" he cried, this time with conviction.

I reached for him and pulled him close to my chest. I was scared to ask him anything more, fearful of what he might say next. I just rocked him back and forth in my arms, hoping to calm us both. I looked up at Brian, who had come into the room to make sure I had sunscreen for my trip. He had heard it too.

I could see on his face the emotions that were palpitating through my own heavy heart.

I didn't want my child to run away. I knew it was a metaphor. I knew Charlie meant that he didn't want to be Charlie anymore. The knot in my stomach grew even bigger. It was hard to swallow. This couldn't be true, but we couldn't pretend we didn't hear it. The words hung heavily in the air over my head as Brian handed me the sunscreen he had found. I took it from him and walked out the door to go to my birthday celebration.

My relaxing spa birthday party was anything but relaxing. I spent the whole time with my girlfriends going over and over the incident with Charlie.

"You guys, you have no idea what that felt like to hear my son say 'Mommy, Charlie ran away.' What the heck does that even mean?!"

They tried their best to reassure me that I was probably reading too much into Charlie's comment about running away. My friend Erin, always there to talk me off a ledge, looked me in the eye.

"It's too early for them to run away. Doesn't that start happening when they are like fifteen or something?"

I looked back at her, and her half-smile told me that that was supposed to be a joke. She then reached over and stroked my arm then, turning more serious.

"For real though, he's three and a half. Just love him. He just needs love right now. Try not to freak out yet."

She squeezed my hand and tipped her mimosa towards mine for a "cheers."

I listened to my friends go back and forth with their viewpoints and explanations and waited for a wave of relief to wash over me, but such relief never came.

I couldn't calm my mind or my heart because all I could feel was a true sense of fear throughout my body. I was okay with my child being unique. I didn't want my child to be a carbon copy of others or a follower of the group for that matter, but to think that my child would be so different that he might be completely misunderstood by most and ultimately rejected? All because of who he was at his core? Parents all want their children to be happy and to feel like they belong somewhere. I just couldn't fathom that my child might not ever belong anywhere. I didn't know much about transgender or gender-fluid children and what it might be like for them growing up so different from others, but I could make an educated guess. So many of my gay friends had told me of their struggles to fit in and be accepted throughout their childhoods. It wasn't the same experience—sexuality versus identity—but there was a parallel. Members of marginalized groups of people often had a rough go in society. Worse, sometimes these people are victims of violence or hate crimes. I remember how horrified and sad I felt when I heard about the murder of Matthew Shepard. He was a gay student attending the University of Wyoming who was beaten, tortured, and left to die back in 1998 because he was gay. I knew that people sometimes fear what they do not understand, but I couldn't even consider these possibilities for my baby.

I thought about what Charlie meant when he said he wanted to run away and never come back. He probably felt that no one understood him for how he felt on the inside. People saw him as a boy named Charlie, and that's not how he wanted to be seen. "Charlie" was standing in the way of my child being his true self. If Charlie ran away, the person who was left behind could become *that* version of himself—the person that he was on the inside. Ultimately, he wanted what we all want: to be accepted for who we truly are.

Still, I didn't know how exactly to move forward. I knew I loved him. I knew I wanted him to be happy. It dawned on me that if I didn't find some sense of understanding of Charlie, I would risk losing my child for real.

CHAPTER NINE

I knew that before Charlie was to enter preschool for the first time, I had to find a professional who would help us navigate the social anxieties that plagued my mind when I thought about my gender "confused" child entering the school system. I needed Google to guide me to the person who could hold our hand and say that everything would be okay.

I opened my laptop and consulted Google. I typed in several configurations: "child therapist for gender-fluid children in San Diego." "Gender non-conforming child therapist San Diego." "Child Psychologist gender identity." One name kept coming up in most of the searches: a woman named Darlene. She was a licensed clinical social worker. I decided to email her to see if she could help us.

Darlene responded that evening. She suggested meeting with Brian and me alone first before meeting Charlie. I told her I was eager to hear her advice, but I didn't know if I was even ready to have my child meet a therapist at three and a half years old. We decided on a date and time, and Darlene emailed me her address. I hadn't realized until then that the location of the office was not published online. Finding it strange, I wrote her back asking why.

"For safety reasons," was her reply.

I grew nervous. *Safety reasons?* Did she mean to say she feared violence of some sort? What did this mean for Charlie? For us? I was apprehensive, but Brian and I were resolved to do right by our child. Seeking professional guidance was part of our commitment to him. I swallowed hard as I wrote the appointment date in my calendar reluctantly.

The day of the appointment with Darlene, I had a whole slew of questions for her. I knew I could talk freely and openly since we had agreed not to bring Charlie to the first appointment. I knew I might get emotional, though I really wasn't prepared to do that in front of a stranger. Neither Brian nor I had ever been to a therapist before.

Darlene's office was in a large old house in a very nice neighborhood in San Diego. After some trepidation, we entered through a gate around the back of the house and let ourselves inside, where there was a sitting area with several chairs gathered around a coffee table littered with magazines and books.

I quickly scanned the book titles stacked on the table. "Beyond Magenta: Transgender Teens Speak Out" and "Raising Ryland: Our Story of Parenting A Transgender Child With No Strings Attached" and "The Transgender Child: A Handbook For Families And Professionals" were some of the titles on the top of the pile. I could feel the tears starting to well up in my eyes just as the door opened at the end of the hallway and a woman with shoulder length blond hair welcomed us in.

I carefully looked her over. She was younger than I had imagined and pretty. Did she have a transgender or gender-fluid child? Is that where her journey had begun? I knew she was a licensed professional with a master's degree, but what real-world experience did she have with a child like ours besides information she had read in books? I hadn't even shaken her hand yet, and I was already on the defensive. *Give her a chance*, I told myself. She smiled warmly when she greeted us.

"Hi, there. I'm Darlene. You must be Brian and Tasha."

She seemed sincere and welcoming. I let my guard down just for a moment and extended my hand to shake hers. "Yes, I'm Tasha, Charlie's mom. It's nice to meet you," I said, looking her in the eye. I wanted to be polite, of course, but I also intended to show her that I was not up for any BS regarding my child.

She turned and led us down the hallway to her office and shut the door behind us. After we all sat down, she asked a very simple question: "So, why are you here today?"

The floodgates opened. For the next fifty minutes, I talked nonstop. Brian interjected here and there, but for the most part, I just babbled on. I told her about potty training and how Charlie said he didn't want a penis. I told her about Charlie's obsession with witches and long hair and about his affinity for all female characters. Darlene listened intently and never interrupted. Finally, in the last five minutes of the session, I stopped to ask her the question I needed answered more than any other. I looked her in the eyes and, with all seriousness, said, "Do you think my child is transgender or not?"

Darlene, with all her professional experience, didn't seem completely taken aback. Carefully, she responded, "Well, he certainly could be, but I really need to meet with him before I can make an assertion of that kind."

You don't know? So what was this appointment even for? I thought to myself. But I knew it was really meant for me to be comfortable—with the idea of a therapist and with the idea of Darlene talking to Charlie. She was right. How could she tell me something so serious about my child when she hadn't even met him yet? My stories were not enough.

We scheduled a meeting with Darlene and Charlie the following week.

I wasn't sure at first how to explain to Charlie who Darlene was or why we were going to see her. I even wondered if I should lie and say we were going to the doctor. But we were going to be in a room with toys, books, and couches—not exactly the same as his pediatrician's office. Charlie was really smart. I didn't want him to sense my trepidation regarding the appointment with Darlene and wonder if there was something wrong. He would ask too many questions, and I wouldn't know how to answer them. I might burst into tears.

My mom suggested that we tell him that we were going to see a nice lady who wanted to talk to him and play for a bit. Darlene had prepped us that she uses play interaction with toys to get the children to feel comfortable and at ease for conversation. So, I went with that. I approached him about an hour before we were set to meet at Darlene's office. "Hey, Charlie?" I started off, trying my best to sound casual. He looked up at me with his brown eyes and said, "Yes, Mommy?" "We are going to go see a nice lady. She has some really fun toys to play with, like trucks and dinosaurs. It will be a lot of fun." I eased into the next part, anticipating some questions in response. "Then she's just going to ask you a few questions. Okay?" Without hesitation, he said, "Okay, Mommy." I was shocked that there was no skepticism from Charlie at all. Just another "play date" to him. It had been so much easier than I had predicted. I took my dad along with us so that Charlie could sit in the lobby with him while Brian and I had a quick chat with Darlene in her office.

She showed us some activities she was going to go over with him. One was a type of questionnaire for kids, with drawings on the pages. As I read it over, my heart started to race.

The paper had rudimentary drawings of people throughout, pink for female and blue for male. One of the questions to consider read something like, "I feel like a girl in my heart and brain," or "I feel like a boy in my heart and brain." Another further down said, "The name I want people to call me is ____________."

This freaked me out. What was Charlie going to say? I wasn't prepared for this brutal honesty…at least not yet. He had said to me so many times already that he was a girl. I feared that if he said it in front of this professional, it would make it that much more official. My boy could be gone for good. But it was too late to back out now. We were already in her office, Charlie was waiting to come in, and I would be writing her a check no matter what. It was now or never.

Darlene opened the door, and I went to get Charlie. I managed to smile but my expression hardly matched what I was feeling inside. My anxiety was through the roof. Charlie entered the room slowly with a quizzical look on his face. He was silent, which was completely out of character. I could tell that he was unsure as to why we were at this strange office to "play," but once he saw the toys, his comfort level completely changed.

"Mommy, look at the dinosaurs! Cars! Yay!" he exclaimed as he started to grab toys from the baskets in Darlene's cubby.

Darlene kneeled on the floor next to him and said, "Oh Charlie, do you like dinosaurs? That's great. Which one is your favorite?"

Charlie grinned widely and held up the blue T-Rex. "Oh, this one!" He exclaimed excitedly.

Charlie and Darlene played on the floor with the dinosaurs together for a couple of minutes until she asked him to come and sit on the couch to talk. He climbed onto the couch next to Darlene, across from Brian and me. Darlene told Charlie that she was going to ask him some questions. She told him that when we meet people, they don't always know if we are a boy or a girl. We must sometimes tell them who we are. He looked at her with rapt attention, as if he was truly processing and understanding every word she said. She took out the paper she had shown us before Charlie came in, the one with the pink girl and blue boy and all the questions about the heart and brain. Obviously, he couldn't read it himself, so she held it up in front of him and started to read.

"Charlie, tell me which one is the way you feel," she instructed. He nodded and she began with the line at the very top. "I have a boy body but feel like a girl in my heart and brain."

Then she went to the next line. "I have a boy body and feel like a boy in my heart and brain."

After she finished reading the second line, she looked at Charlie and said, "Which one is you, Charlie?"

He paused for maybe ten seconds and then said, "girl in my heart and brain."

My eyes opened wide. My heart leapt into my throat. I looked at Brian to see that his face had gone white. Darlene kept going. "What name would you like for your mommy and daddy to call you?"

Again, a tiny pause from Charlie and then he blurted, "Room on the Broom!"

He had the biggest smile on his face. Darlene was knowledgeable about the *Room on the Broom* book and his obsession with it. "Okay, Room on the Broom, thank you."

She talked to him for some time after this, asking him how he felt about himself, what made him happy, which other characters in his stories he liked the most, and he answered as best as a three-and-a-half-year-old could. I was only half listening at that point because it felt like the room was closing in, and my heart and mind were racing. Darlene concluded her talk with Charlie and then escorted him out to be with Grandpa. Then she closed the door and sat down to finish the meeting with us.

"What are you both thinking and feeling right now?" Darlene asked us as she sat down across from us on the couch.

I didn't even know where to start.

"So ... he feels like a girl then?" Brian asked.

"Yeah, does this mean he's transgender then?" I said before Darlene could respond. "I mean, oh, god!"

"Well, to be honest," she said carefully, "it certainly sounds like that is what we have here."

"Transgender then?" I shot back. "You asked him a couple of questions! How can we declare something so big after a few questions and not even a half an hour with him? He's not even four!"

I wasn't quite yelling, but I had significantly raised my voice. Darlene's eyebrows moved upwards, but she appeared to remain calm.

"Tasha," she said, "I'm not pronouncing him transgender. He is still very young; you are right, but in my experience, a child would not declare so easily that their body doesn't match up with how they feel in their heart and brain if it were not, in fact, true. Remember, you must also ask yourself about Charlie's behavior, is it persistent and consistent?"

I had heard this before from her, in our last meeting. It was a common indicator for transgender children.

I looked at Brian to save me—from Darlene, from myself, from this situation. I could tell that he was also struggling to process everything that had happened in her office. It was like the whole world had changed inside of an hour.

"So, it's possible for him to still not be transgender," Brian finally said. "This isn't like a full-fledged 'diagnosis' or something? It could still be a phase of some sort?"

It was almost as if he was begging now.

Darlene let out a slight sigh. "Of course, anything is still possible. I'm just giving you my professional opinion. And I must ask, would it really be so bad if he were transgender?"

I wanted to fling open her office door and run screaming from the room. I never wanted to come back to this place. She was trying to put my child in a box, a marginalized box, a box that would mean a much harder life for my child. My mind flashed back to Matthew Shepard. I could feel the anger and fear rising inside me. It was all I could manage to look her in the eye and respond.

"We would love Charlie no matter who he is, but I can't talk about this anymore." I managed to reach into my purse for her check, feeling in that moment that she was not only taking money from me, but she was also stealing something else from me along with it.

Darlene took the check when I handed it to her. As Brian and I stood to go, she got up as well.

"Should we make another appointment then?" she asked.

I glanced quickly at Brian and could tell in two seconds that he felt exactly the way I did. The tension in the room was palpable.

"No, I think we are fine for now. Thanks," was all I could muster.

"Okay," she replied, "Just reach out if you need something."

She shut the door behind us, and we walked solemnly to the lobby to get Charlie and Grandpa. I couldn't wait to put this building—and Darlene—in our rearview mirror.

Brian and I did not speak a word on our ride home from Darlene's office. Grandpa and Charlie chatted away quietly in the backseat, remarking on everything they saw pass by outside the window. I was grateful for the white noise as a small distraction. My mind was racing with so many thoughts, and it felt as though my heart was going to beat out of my chest. Brian and I stole a few glances at each other as we rode along. I contemplated jumping out of the car and running as fast as I could away from this situation, away from my life, but I reminded myself that Brian was in this too. I couldn't run away from this any more than he could.

When we got back to our house, Grandpa took Charlie inside to play with Legos, leaving Brian and me to stew together in the car. As soon as we were alone, I went off.

"Brian, what the hell?!" I screamed much too loudly from the passenger seat. "I'm so pissed! She barely even talked to him! How in the hell can she say that he's transgender?" I said these words even though that was exactly what my gut had been telling me he was for some time.

Brian, naturally, was a bit calmer than I was, but I could still feel his frustration in his words.

"Yeah, I am not sure about her at all," he said. "Obviously, if he were transgender, that would be good business for her. I'm not saying she's lying, but it was damn quick to basically diagnose a three-and-a-half-year-old child! How can she have been thorough with her assessment?"

Brian may not have been as convinced by Darlene, but he wasn't as angry as I was.

"Well," I fired back, "we are not going back there. I just feel like she asked him leading questions, and basically *wanted* him to say he feels like a girl. Come on! Maybe right now he does, but that could change in a few months. Give me a break, lady!"

Brian grabbed my hand, and I could see from his look that I had come unhinged.

"Like I've said before, honey, we need to just follow Charlie's lead. Let's take this one day at a time. There are a lot of things going on with him, and we just need to figure it out ourselves. We don't need to listen to everything Darlene says."

I nodded in response, though I was still unconvinced. After a deep breath, I finally stepped out of our car.

Charlie, for one, seemed to be unfazed by the experience with Darlene. While Brian and I grappled with our thoughts and feelings about the present and future, he pressed forward with his love of dolls, female cartoon characters, and long hair. He turned up the volume on the female pronoun usage, correcting us all the time. My child had ears like a hawk, and it caught me off guard all the time. I would ask Brian a question in the kitchen, referring to Charlie as "he," and little Charlie would suddenly appear out of nowhere and say, "Mommy, I'm a she!"

"Oh, Charlie, I'm sorry," I'd say, still avoiding the pronoun even when I was being admonished.

"Say *she*, Mommy," Charlie scolded, not willing to let me off the hook. Through gritted teeth, I looked at him and said, "*She*." I held my child's gaze until he left the room, then I let out a small scoff and rolled my eyes.

I looked to Brian and whispered, "How did he—*she*—hear me? Good lord!"

Brian had a dejected look on his face and just shrugged in response. I was still not willing to fully give in.

A couple days later, on a routine trip to Costco, my emotional fortitude was put to the test in a new way. Oliver sat in the cart Brian was pushing, and I walked slightly behind them, holding Charlie's hand. We were headed towards the wine section when I saw, up ahead on the right-hand side, in the middle of the store, two large racks of girls' summer dresses.

I felt my body flinch. A pit formed in my stomach. In what felt like an involuntary motion, I grabbed the side of the cart and turned it sharply to the left. Brian let out a loud "Hey!" before I could say anything to warn him.

After I successfully turned the cart in the opposite direction of the dresses, I spoke succinctly and firmly. "We need to go in this direction *now*."

Brian whipped his head around to look. He turned back around and simply said, "Yes, I understand."

It was then that I finally looked down at Charlie to see if he knew what had just happened. Thankfully, he seemed to only be looking forward, towards the surfboards and kayaks we were quickly approaching. He had not said a word about the dresses—he had not seen them. We had dodged a bullet in my mind. He had never said anything about wearing a dress, but my mother's intuition just knew. If he had seen the dresses, I knew he would have begged me for one. We had been skirting around the edge of female clothing for some time, and I knew that that would be next. I had found ways to explain to our friends why Charlie was wearing a blanket on his head (he loves to pretend!) or why he continued to tell everyone he was Room on the Broom (it's his favorite book!), but if he wore a dress, I'd be forced to explain what was really going on with our child, that he might not, in fact, be a boy. I couldn't bear to say no to him, but I knew I didn't want to say yes either.

Over the weeks that followed, I mulled over the Darlene meeting. While I didn't agree with her absolute assessment of my child, I was grateful for some small takeaways. I realized that Charlie was still really attached to the *Room on the Broom* character. I also realized that it wasn't right of me to keep that book away from him. If the book brought him joy, how could I justify hiding it? I knew I needed to return it to him.

While Charlie was in the bathtub one night, I snuck into his room and retrieved *Room on the Broom* from its secure hiding spot high in his closet. I laid it on his dresser and went back to the bathroom to fetch him from the tub.

Charlie saw the book immediately upon entering his bedroom.

"Mommy!" He cried as he rushed over to put his hands on the book.

"It's back! *Room on the Broom* is back!" He looked at me suddenly with curious eyes. "I thought you took it away!"

He was more inquiring than accusatory with this statement, but I instantly felt ashamed. How could I have kept a *book* away from my beautiful child? What was wrong with me?

"Oh, honey, I'm sorry. I just wanted us to read other things for a while," I tried to explain with a wavering voice. "But it's back now. I'm glad you are happy," I managed to finish.

"Mommy, yes! I'm so excited! I love *Room on the Broom*!"

His pure joy and excitement about the book was unmistakable. I was shocked that he wasn't upset with me for withholding it—instead, it was like I had made his day. In that moment, I felt like the worst and best parent at the same time.

"I'm Room on the Broom!" he squealed as he danced around the bedroom with the book clutched tightly to his chest.

Here we go again, I thought. At least he was smiling. (That meant I did the right thing in the end, right?)

I then read the book aloud for what was probably the two-hundredth time.

I wasn't exactly sure how I felt about having Room on the Broom back in our lives. Part of me was happy to see my child happy. The other part of me was weary. I felt that by giving in to my child's happiness, I had taken the lid completely off Pandora's box. As I watched him dance around our living room with a baby blanket perched on his head underneath his witch's hat—beaming—I had to wonder. Though I was deeply ashamed that I had sacrificed my child's happiness by hiding the book, admittedly I was more concerned with what would happen now that I had given it back.

As parents, we say we wish for nothing more than for our children to be happy. That's true, but sometimes we are tested. Sometimes when we, as parents, are uncomfortable with something our children are choosing to do—or be—we just want them to stop, for our sake. We temporarily forget about their happiness. We selfishly consider only our own state of being. We do this irrationally. I was so overwhelmed by Charlie's behavior and declarations of identity that I could only think about how sad and uncomfortable it made *me* feel.

I could say that I wanted him to be happy, but when I began to think about what would truly make him happy—allowing him to act like a girl or dress like a girl or, God forbid, *be* a girl—I wanted that all to go away for me. And every time I allowed him to have one more girl toy or agreed to use the feminine pronouns or let him pretend to have long hair, I felt more and more uncomfortable and out of control.

I wanted him to be happy. I really did.

I just didn't know how both of us could be happy at the same time.

As time went on, I felt submerged in the shame and embarrassment of my child. I was frustrated with myself. My child needed me to be a role model, a pillar of strength, and a guide to the truth, but I was struggling with what the truth really was.

I had so much fear and anxiety surrounding my child's behavior and possibly inevitable future that I felt like I was walking around in a fog daily. Charlie was my firstborn. With his birth, he had made me into a mother. Was it too much to ask that he just be an average child?

Why did all this confusion and fear have to come with this beautifully magical experience?

One night towards the end of summer, I was flipping through the channels with Brian as I sipped a glass of Chianti. Then I saw it, *Frozen*, the movie. As I stared at the screen, my anxiety levels suddenly spiked. It felt like my heart might beat out of my chest.

Brian looked over at me, seemingly confused.

"What's up, babe? That's that cute movie that everyone has been talking about forever, isn't it? I hate that song though. What is it, "Let It Go" or something cheesy? Drives me crazy. But I bet the kids would love it," he quipped. He paused for a half second, then said, "Well, I know Charlie would love it. Look at that Princess!"

He pointed to the main character, Elsa, and smiled. "She even has a long braid like Room on the Broom!" I knew he was joshing me a little. He could sense my apprehension but also wanted me to lighten up a bit.

I finally looked at him.

"Oh, hell no," I said. "I'm not letting Charlie watch that movie. Are you kidding me?"

He was up for the challenge. "Honey, why not? It's a cartoon. He would love it. Really, what am I not getting?"

I took a deep breath and collected my thoughts.

"Yes, he would love it—that's the problem. I know that sounds crazy, but I don't think I could handle it. I think he would love it so much that there would be no turning back. He'd want to be that Elsa princess, and there would be no end to it. My Charlie would really be gone. He already said Charlie ran away. But my Charlie is still here on some level, and I need that to remain. I'm not sure about a lot of things right now, but I am sure that I cannot let Charlie watch this movie, at least not yet. I hope you can respect my thought process." Charlie had pretended to be various girl characters in stories and shows for some time; that was not new. He had been Princess Pea, Emily the Train, Room on the Broom, of course, but no character was quite as convincing—as a true female person—as this Elsa in *Frozen*. It was too close to being reality.

I finished my speech and turned away from Brian, exhausted. Brian grabbed my hand.

"Okay, honey. I understand."

Even if he didn't understand, he was willing to put up with my crazy ideas for a bit longer.

Later, when I was alone, my guilt propelled me to grab the remote. Without really thinking, I clicked back through the channel guide and found a time the next day when *Frozen* would be shown again. Almost involuntarily, I clicked the record button. There. Now I wasn't such a bad mother. I wasn't going to let my son watch Frozen—not yet—but at least I wasn't banning it completely from our household. Once it was on the DVR, I could decide *if* and when to let Charlie watch it. No pressure. It would be there waiting until I was ready.

I just had no idea when that might be.

CHAPTER TEN

"Mommy, where are we going?" Charlie asked me with a solemn face. I swallowed the lump in my throat and looked him straight in the eye. Somehow, I managed to smile.

"Well, honey, we are getting a haircut. I mean, it's really more of a trim. Just the ends. For school."

I hoped he couldn't hear the fear and hesitation in my broken sentences. Shockingly, he didn't respond. Instead, he entered the door when I opened it and walked right in.

As we approached the end of August, we began to prepare Charlie to start preschool for the first time. For so long it had just been Charlie and his nanny, Margarita, and then Charlie and my parents. I was excited for him to finally engage with other children his own age on a regular basis.

Part of me was excited. The other part was terrified. I was worried that he would present with his gender-fluid behavior at this school—which was in a church, no less—and that he would be teased, or worse, rejected. I wanted to embrace him for who he was, but at the same time, I wanted desperately to protect him from any negativity that might come at him. One of the things I had to consider was his hair. It had been a couple of months since I had cut it. It was borderline shaggy surfer style, but if I let it grow any longer, people would confuse him for a girl.

I needed to buy myself more time.

I hadn't told Charlie that we were going to get a haircut until the minute before we walked into the Super Cuts. He was almost four at this point and very aware. As we approached the salon, a confused look flashed across his face. I knew he didn't want to cut his hair. This was going to be bad.

I told the lady at the counter that we wanted a trim so he could be ready for school. I thought if I phrased it that way, maybe Charlie would think that the school required this sort of thing, that I was simply following the rules. I caught myself holding my breath as we walked to the chair. Charlie climbed up to sit on the booster seat in the salon chair and looked at me with his big brown eyes.

"Mommy, this is the last time we cut my hair," he said, without breaking my gaze.

There was a maturity in the way he spoke, a sense of knowing more than he should know at this age.

I didn't argue. I couldn't.

He was pleading with me in his own way, while also abiding by my request. It would have broken my heart to say anything other than, "Okay, honey, this is the last time."

I smiled at the hairdresser as she approached and our conversation was over.

I let her take off only an inch, so when he walked out of Super Cuts, Charlie was still sporting a longish haircut—for a boy. It was a compromise for now.

I was anxious to see what the school's reaction to my child would be in just two weeks' time. As usual, Brian tried his best to reassure me.

"Honey, we don't need to say anything to the teacher, at least not now. He's Charlie, and what he does or says at home isn't guaranteed to be replicated at school. We should wait and see, not freak people out before we really know."

He was calm in his delivery, but I knew that he, too, was nervous about this Presbyterian school and how exactly they would handle a gender-fluid child. I believed Presbyterian churches to be a bit more open-minded than other denominations of Christianity, and this specific church to be even more so. I had friends who attended the church and could vouch for that aspect, but it was still a church, and bible studies would be taught once a week in the classroom. I knew there would be an implied right and wrong. I wondered which side of the morality line Charlie and our family would fall on. Would we be judged for *allowing* our child to present with a fluid gender identity?

Thankfully, my fears were assuaged on the first day. Right away we felt comfortable at the preschool. Mandy and Jenna, Charlie's two teachers, seemed unfazed by Charlie's longer hairstyle, and they didn't bat an eye when he showed up at school wearing pink shoes or wanting to play dress-up in actual dresses. Kids this age were notorious for experimenting with toys and clothes of either gender; I knew that better than anyone. A lot of progressive parenting books instructed parents to raise their kids with more gender-neutral toys and clothes—to not let society put your child in a box, so to speak.

But even with all these modern ideas becoming popular, my maternal instinct told me that I needed to at least start a conversation with Mandy and Jenna about my child's proclivities. First and foremost, I didn't want my child to be teased or ridiculed. But admittedly, I was also afraid of Brian and I being judged. I was worried people might think something was wrong with Charlie, and I was also worried they thought Brian and I might have done something to cause it.

A month into preschool, I felt that I needed to get ahead of it in case the teachers were privy to more about Charlie than I realized. If we could at least explain ourselves, Jenna and Mandy would see that we were just a different sort of normal.

When I walked into my meeting with Mandy, I was nervous and wary. I had no idea what I would say, nor did I know what she might say in return. I sat down awkwardly on a child-sized chair facing Mandy in the center of the room.

"Thank you for coming in, Tasha," she said as she smiled warmly at me. "I understand you have some concerns about Charlie that you wanted to discuss with me?"

"Uh, yes," I stammered. "Well, I'm sure you can see by now that Charlie is a unique and different little boy—he's not like the others."

I finished my sentence clumsily and could feel the perspiration forming at my hairline. *God, it is hot in this room!* I thought. *Why don't they open the windows?*

Mandy just looked at me and continued to smile. I could tell she wanted me to finish my thoughts.

"Charlie has always been, you know, more feminine, I guess."

Mandy waited some more.

"He, well… " I paused for a second to breathe before I launched into it. "He has told us a few times now that he is a girl. But, you know, we don't really know what that means. We know he is a different kind of boy, and we love him—of course! We just don't know what is going to happen in the future."

I was talking fast now, just wanting to get it all out there before I lost my nerve. "I guess I just wanted to tell you in case he said something to you like that—I mean, *has* he said something like that to you?"

I was finally out with it. I had come clean with the whole shebang. There was no turning back now.

I looked at Mandy with trepidation. She waited a few seconds before she responded.

"Charlie is wonderful. Jenna and I could tell that he has a softer side. We love that about him. He is so good with the other kids, so patient and kind. But yes, he did say something to me once. It was more of a 'Miss Mandy, I want to be like a girl someday,' comment or something. I just nodded and went on with the project we were working on. He didn't say it again."

I felt a need to defend him then, though Mandy was not disparaging or judging my child at that moment.

"Oh. Okay. Well, he didn't do anything wrong, and I hope that if he says it again and another child says something mean, you will stop that from happening, right?" I pleaded with her to help me.

"Oh yes, of course we would. We are here to help in any way we can. We want all our children to get along and to respect each other. That's what we are here for." She seemed a bit uncomfortable with the topic but was still able to be reassuring and diplomatic.

I had one more request to make of her. Instead of allowing my fear to quash the concern in my mind, I forged ahead, blurting out the question I was most fearful of hearing the answer to.

"What if Charlie ends up wanting to wear a dress to school? I mean, he hasn't asked to yet, so he might never do it, but if he did, I mean—would you be okay with it? Would you embrace it? Or, I guess, allow it, even?"

I had been looking away from Mandy as I formed this question, but my eyes landed firmly on hers once I had managed to get it all out. It felt like an eternity passed as we sat across from each other, just staring. This was obviously a first for her as a teacher. I couldn't blame her for being confused or uneasy with this situation. *But I would. I would blame her.*

She held my child's first experience with social acceptance in her hands. What she said and did in this moment would dictate if we stayed at this preschool or chose to go. So much was on the line in those few seconds of silence.

When Mandy finally spoke, it was once again with a soft smile on her pretty face. "If wearing a dress to school is something that Charlie wants to do, just let me know. We want Charlie to be happy, and we will do whatever we can to make that happen."

I finally let out the air in my lungs and breathed. I smiled back at Mandy and managed to utter, "Thank you, Mandy."

I knew I would cry if I said anything more. I left Mandy's room with a huge sense of relief. I tried not to think about what exactly the other parents would say about seeing Charlie in a dress or what exactly the teachers would choose to tell them about my child in response. I couldn't engage in those thoughts now. I was just grateful that Mandy was on board with helping to make Charlie feel welcome and comfortable, no matter what gender he presented.

I made it all the way to my car in the parking lot with tears welling up in my eyes and a lump in my throat. As soon as my keys met the lock on the door, I burst into tears. I bawled all the way home.

A couple weeks went by after that hopeful meeting with Mandy, and we found ourselves back at Costco, smack dab in the middle of the store. Before I realized where we were, there were little girls' frilly dresses in every direction I turned. I frantically looked for an escape route but there wasn't a clear option in sight. The expression on Charlie's face could only be described as pure joy.

Right then I knew I had to acquiesce and buy him a dress. I was going to buy my son his first dress. He was going to wear a dress. But only in my house. I would not let him wear it anywhere else. That was my compromise.

"Okay, Charlie, we can get you one. To wear *at home*," I managed to speak while glancing sideways at Brian.

He had a resigned look on his face—he didn't have it in him to fight the outcome that day. Charlie seemed okay with my answer, not trying to insist on wearing the dress elsewhere. He was elated just to have a dress.

"Mommy, I want the purple one! This is pretty!" He squealed with excitement as he pawed at the purple organza dress with pink ribbons.

"Okay, that is Rapunzel's dress. From the Disney movie," I trailed off, knowing that he had not yet seen it.

"Oh, yes, Mommy! I love it. Can I get it? Can I?" His face was jubilant and hopeful. As hard as this was for me, I loved seeing him this happy.

"Yes, we can Charlie. Let's find your size," I said as I rummaged through the rack to find a size four.

I kept the dress in the cart, not wanting anyone to know that the dress was, in fact, for my son. I was glad he was happy, but I was also trying to save myself the embarrassment. I hoped the checkout guy would think the dress was for my niece or some other non-family member. Charlie didn't seem to notice my apprehension. He practically skipped to the checkout line.

When we got home, Charlie raced to the bathroom, leaving a trail of clothes behind him.

"Mommy, put the dress on me!" He shrieked in my direction. Reluctantly, I followed and helped him put the purple dress on over his head.

Once he had it on, he looked very cute. With his hair a little longish and this dress on, he could quite easily pass for a girl. *Well, here we go*, I thought, and took a deep breath.

"Picture, Mommy, picture!" Charlie insisted, reaching for my phone. With a catch in my throat, I snapped a couple pictures of him posing in the dress. I was thinking to myself at that moment, *this is my baby's first dress.*

I was emotionally exhausted after Charlie's dress day. I put him to bed that night and solemnly walked to my bedroom. I just wanted to be alone. As I sat down on my side of the bed, I caught a glimpse of a book on the nightstand. Hidden underneath some magazines, I could just barely read the title on the spine. *Raising My Rainbow*, it read.

Oh god, I'd almost forgotten about that one. I bought it months ago, intending to read it to gain some clarity regarding Charlie's behavior. This memoir was about a mother coming to terms with raising a gender-fluid child, all the ups and downs that come with something like that. But by the time it had arrived in the mail, I didn't want anything to do with it. I didn't want to know anything about the author or her gender-fluid child. I didn't have the strength to hear about the child's potential bullying or the mother's obvious struggles with the situation.

When I ordered it, I thought the book might bring me insight. I thought it could help me to understand my child better. But reading the book would mean that I might have to admit similarities between this child and my own. At the time, I hadn't been ready to accept any resemblance between the two children. I had pleaded with my mom to read it first. She would tell me if I could handle it, if I was, in fact, ready. My mother read the book in a couple of days. When she brought it back to me, I knew from the look on her face that now was not the time. She didn't have to say much when she handed it over. "Don't read it yet," she said, grasping my hand while she said it. She quickly turned away so I wouldn't see her eyes well up with tears. That had been three months ago.

I slipped the book out from under the magazines and read the jacket cover again. I ran my hand over the smooth surface of the top cover and took a deep breath. After the day we'd had with the dress, I felt mostly numb, but I had found a glimmer of strength inside myself while at Costco. I had survived. And though I didn't quite understand it all, I knew my child was happy. Maybe I could read this book now after all. I would read it in sections, I told myself, and if it got too hard, I could always put it down. I sat back on the bed and opened the book to the first page.

I didn't put the book down for at least a couple of hours.

Everything was snowballing all around me. First letting Charlie's hair grow long, then switching to female pronouns at home, buying him a dress, and reading *Raising my Rainbow*, I was doing my best to roll with the changes, but I still felt like I was a boat caught in a storm, without any kind of anchor.

I was flipping through my DVR a few days after starting the book. I was almost through with it and feeling emotionally numb. I caught a glimpse of the movie that I had forgotten I had taped months before, *Frozen*. I had taped it because I knew deep in my heart that Charlie would love it. I had taped it because at the time I was not ready to witness how much he would love it. My fear was that if he saw the beautiful princess in the movie, he would likely do everything he could to emulate her. It was just too much for me at the time.

But so much had happened recently that now I thought, *What is one more thing?* Charlie was happy, and this was bound to make him even happier. I mustered up the courage and called Charlie into the living room.

"Charlie! Er, Room on the Broom! Come here, honey. I have something to show you," I called into the next room.

Charlie bounded over to me wearing his Rapunzel dress and said, "What is it, Mommy?"

"It is a movie that I taped for you. It's called *Frozen*, and it is about an ice princess named Elsa," I said carefully, trying not to lose my nerve.

His eyes immediately lit up. "Yay! Let's watch it!" He jumped up and down while he shrieked at the top of his lungs.

I pushed play on the DVR and took several deep breaths, waiting for my heart to stop racing. The movie captivated him instantly, just like I knew it would. I had to admit that I was pretty captivated as well. This Elsa character was no joke. She wasn't the waif-y, weak princess of the old days that was waiting for a prince to save her. She was strong, independent, smart, and beautiful. I was impressed. Disney had upped their game significantly with this movie. As for the song, "Let it Go"? Well, it was actually kind of catchy. Elsa sang it with strength and power. It was all about letting go of who she used to be and embracing her real self.

Wow. Was this some kind of weird prophecy meant for our family? I had no idea this cartoon would affect me in such a profound way.

As soon as the credits rolled, Charlie looked at me with a huge smile and said, "Mommy, call me Elsa!"

Oh, Lord, of course, I thought.

Well, if he was going to be a Disney princess, this was the one I would want him to be.

"Okay, Elsa," I said, catching Brian's eye across the room.

I wanted my Charlie back, but I figured Elsa was better—and easier to say—than Room on the Broom. Charlie skipped out of the room to find something to make a braid in his hair like Elsa the ice princess.

"Babe, so we have to call him Elsa now?" Brian rolled his eyes while he asked me this.

I knew it was crazy, but I didn't have much left in me to fight it.

"Yeah, I guess. I knew he wouldn't take no for an answer, and you have to admit, that Elsa chick is quite the lady. She's feisty and tough. That's how I'd want my girl to be."

I said "my girl" because I had a feeling I knew where this was all headed.

"All right, honey," Brian responded as he stood up. "Mommy knows best, but I still kind of hate that song."

He walked out of the room. It was my turn to roll my eyes.

We were adjusting as best we could to having a princess in the house. I was still reading *Raising my Rainbow* and wondering if I was raising my own girly boy—like the mother in the book described her son to be—or if Charlie was going to turn out to be something entirely different.

We had rules about the Princess dress. Charlie could wear it whenever he wanted to at home. I felt like it was a nice compromise on my part. I was proud of myself when he asked me if he could wear the dress to play outside in our yard, and I said yes. We didn't really know our neighbors, so there wouldn't be a lot of questions regarding why my boy was wearing a dress. I still felt safe. My child felt protected. Then one Saturday I was feeding Oliver outside in his highchair while Charlie was dancing around the driveway in his Rapunzel dress when he approached Brian with a question.

"Daddy, can I ride my tricycle?"

Brian paused and surveyed the driveway. There were three cars parked there, and it was already hard for Charlie to have room to play as it was. I figured Brian would offer to move a couple of the cars so that Charlie would have room to ride his trike.

Instead, he said, "Oh, okay, Charlie, go get it, and we can ride on the sidewalk."

I almost choked on my water as he said this to my son. He sounded confident and unyielding to fear. I panicked and shouted out to Brian as he turned to walk toward the end of the driveway to wait for Charlie.

"Uh, Brian, are you sure? I mean, there are a lot of cracks in the sidewalk. I wouldn't want him to fall off and get hurt." I was grasping for a reason to stop Charlie from going out there so close to the street. Anyone could see him then. He wouldn't be protected. But I was careful not to reveal the true reason for my fear, whilst Charlie might hear. Brian turned and shrugged.

"It will be okay," he said, not convincing me.

"Honey!" I tried another angle with him. "He's too big for that tricycle. Hasn't he outgrown it? Why don't we move the cars, and he can practice riding his bike with the training wheels instead?" I was desperate to stop this situation. I felt so out of control. I needed to keep him in the driveway, away from other people.

"Tasha, we will just go for a little bit. I will be right there next to him. He will be okay." Brian tried to reassure me, as if the cracks in the sidewalk were really my concern.

I couldn't do anything to stop them; they were already at the sidewalk. I couldn't leave Oliver alone in the highchair. I went back to feeding Oliver and tried to wait patiently for them to return.

No more than fifteen minutes later, they were back. Brian looked a little stunned and Charlie a little disappointed. *Oh god, what happened? My baby!* I was reeling inside.

"Honey, is everything okay? Did you guys have fun?" I tried to conceal my worry and focused on downplaying whatever had just taken place on the sidewalk. Brian pulled me to the side out of Charlie's earshot and replayed the scenario for me.

"Well, we went on the other sidewalk, facing Market Street." He started the story.

Market street was fifty times busier than the street in front of our house. That meant so much more visibility, so many more opportunities for people to see my son in a dress. I could feel a lump rising in my throat as I thought about these facts.

"Everything was fine, and then these young boys—damn teenagers—walked up the sidewalk and started pointing and laughing at Charlie."

"Oh, no!" I shrieked, so upset now. "What did you do? Did Charlie know they were laughing at him? What jerks! He's a child for god's sake!"

I was livid. Teenagers were supposed to be more open-minded than adults, right?

Brian was upset but clearly not as upset as I was. "I just glared at them with a really dirty look. I didn't want to say anything in front of Charlie. I was hoping he would not even realize it was about his dress." He stopped for a moment to think. "I think he knew it was directed at him, but he didn't say anything to me except that he was ready to come back to the house."

I was devastated. How could some stupid kids think it was okay to insult my precious baby? He was not quite four years old!

"I knew you shouldn't have gone past the driveway." I said this defensively, but carefully. I didn't want Brian to think I was scolding him.

"Look, it was horrible. I feel bad that it happened. I'm surprised they even knew he was a boy; his hair is longer now. I don't know. They are stupid kids anyway. I don't think Charlie will take it that badly." Brian said this with a hopeful look on his face.

Just as he said it, Charlie blazed around the house past us on his tricycle. His hair was flowing out behind him, and he had a huge grin on his face. Whatever he had experienced on the sidewalk seemed to have rolled right off his back. It seemed that he was not aware of the negativity surrounding the laughter. Charlie had no idea that he could be teased or judged for just being himself. I was okay with him living in this bubble for the time being. Once he figured out how cruel people could be, a bit of his innocence would be stolen.

I was a fool to think that Charlie's riding a bike in his dress would be a one-time thing. About a week after the tricycle confrontation, he was ready to try it again. This time he wanted to ride his new two-wheeler with training wheels rather than the tricycle.

When Charlie approached his dad that Saturday in his Rapunzel dress asking to ride his two-wheeler, I knew that Brian's response might be tinged with hesitation from the sting of his last encounter with Charlie in a dress on a bike.

"Oh, Charlie, honey, I don't know if you should ride your bike with that dress on. It might get caught in the spokes of the wheels and you could fall off and get hurt."

Brian was always safety minded. But this was different. I could see the discomfort in his body language. He was not quite ready for another barrage of laughter coming from strangers directed at his child.

Charlie was immediately distraught. "Daddy, no! I will not fall! My dress is fine! I promise!" Charlie's little face was full of anguish and despair. He pleaded with Brian for him to change his mind.

Brian stuck to his answer. "Charlie, it is a long dress. It is not safe for the bike. How about you take off the dress and ride in your non-dress-up clothes?" Brian tried to reason with him.

Charlie's face was bright red by this point. "NO!" he shouted. "I will not take off this dress! You are mean to me!" Charlie turned on his heel and ran up the stairs back to the house.

I turned to Brian with disbelief. Charlie never raised his voice at us, let alone screamed at the top of his lungs. He had always been calm, patient, sweet-natured. Oliver was the screamer. I didn't know what to think. Brian and I sat in silence staring at each other for several minutes.

Then it dawned on me.

"Brian, oh my god, I think I have figured something out," I started, but then Brian interrupted me.

"It's not like I don't want him to wear the dress. I just really don't want him to get it caught in the bike. It just doesn't make sense to have that long dress hanging down where it could so easily cause him to fall."

"But, honey, that's just it, don't you see?"

Brian looked at me with confusion.

"He's upset not just because you won't let him ride the bike in his dress. I think he's really upset because he thinks you will take the dress away—like for good." I paused so he could digest what I was saying. "I think he is scared that he will lose the dress." It was my mother's intuition screaming inside my brain as to what was happening. I had no choice but to listen.

Brian's face softened. "Oh my, sweetheart. I didn't even think about that." He let out a sigh. "I don't want to take the dress away, you know that." He looked me in the eyes to confirm that I understood his intentions. "He must be so scared to lose something that makes him so happy. I want him to be happy."

"Bless his little heart. Let's go find him and tell him that we will never take the dress away from him if it makes him happy," I managed to reply, just barely above a whisper. If I spoke any louder, the tears might come pouring down my cheeks.

We ascended the stairs up to the house. We found Charlie in our bedroom, sitting on the bare hardwood floor. It was not where I expected to find him. Brian and I sat down on the floor next to him, and at first, no one spoke.

Finally, I said, "Charlie, we love you so much. We just want you to know that this is your dress. We will never take it away from you. Daddy just doesn't want it to get caught in the bike."

I paused to think and then said, "Maybe I could tie up the side of it so that the bottom doesn't hang down by the tires? Then you wouldn't get it caught."

I wanted him to be happy again. I hated seeing him so distraught.

Brian gave Charlie a weak smile and said, "Yeah, honey, we love you, and we love your dress. Daddy doesn't want to take your dress away. We can do what Mommy said and tie your dress up, okay?"

He pleaded with Charlie for some sort of forgiveness, understanding. It seemed like an eternity before Charlie responded. When he finally did, he spoke so quietly that we almost couldn't hear him.

"Mommy, I have a secret, but I'll tell you when I am older."

He was looking at the floor when he said this. My heart sank to my stomach just as my eyes jumped up to meet Brian's. We didn't have to say anything to each other.

We knew what his secret was.

With my heart beating rapidly in my chest, I tried to control my breathing as I looked over at Charlie. "We love you, baby. You can tell us your secret whenever you want to. We love you."

Brian and I looked at each other again. The color had drained from his face. Brian looked at Charlie and said, "Come on, buddy, let's go outside and get your dress situated so you can be safe on your bike."

It took everything I had in me not to completely lose it when Charlie and Brian got up from the floor to leave the room.

CHAPTER ELEVEN

Charlie's fourth birthday was right around the corner. I realized that I really needed to get on the ball with planning a party for him.

"Hey, baby, what would you like to do to celebrate your birthday next month?" I asked.

Charlie paused his coloring project, looking earnestly at his purple crayon. Then his face quickly lit up and he turned to look me in the eyes.

"Mommy!" he shouted, "I want to have a party at Jump Around!"

Jump Around was basically this indoor playground with trampolines, bounce houses, and climbing walls. It was the perfect place to let kids run around and get their energy out and at the same time keep them contained. I was excited that he wanted to go there because it meant no setup or cleanup—we could just show up with a cake and then after two hours of play and food, leave the mess behind.

"Okay, babe," I said, "that sounds good. Who would you like to invite?"

He answered my question almost immediately.

"I want Carter and Conner and James!" He beamed from ear to ear while spouting off the boys' names to me. He had gravitated towards the boys in his class immediately upon the start of preschool and only recently had begun to form some bonds with a couple of little girls there, too.

"Okay, are those the only kids you want? You don't want the whole class there?" He confirmed that he didn't.

I sent out the invitations to the three boys he named.

On the Monday before the big event, I asked Charlie if he was excited for his upcoming party when I picked him up from school.

"Yes, Mommy! Is my whole class coming?" He asked me with big wide eyes as I buckled him in his car seat.

My heart sank. "Oh, honey, no. I only invited Connor, Carter, and James. Those were the kids you told me you wanted. I asked you if you wanted any other kids, and you said no."

"Mommy!" he wailed, "I want all the kids to come to my party! Why didn't you ask them? It's not fair!"

He was on the verge of tears now.

I stepped back from the car to get some space and took a deep breath. *I shouldn't have listened to him*, I thought. *I should have known better. I'm the mom. Why didn't I just invite all the kids anyway?* I already knew the answer.

I didn't want all the kids there.

Too many parents I didn't know.

Too much to worry about.

Too much might be seen that could never be unseen.

As I got in the driver's seat and started the car, I was overcome with guilt. It was too late to invite other kids—the party was in five days. I had to try my best to make Charlie happy under the current circumstances, when deep down I had spent the entire time planning his birthday hoping that he would actually be a boy at the party!

"I'm sorry, baby. I thought you only wanted those boys. I should have asked your whole class anyway. It is my fault. But it is going to be so much fun at Jump Around, and Judah and Chrissy and Alec will be there, too!" I named some of the kids of our adult friends that were coming, hoping it would get him more excited and then he would forget about the other classmates.

I looked in the rearview mirror at my son and saw him nod his head as he continued to look out the window. That was as much approval as I was going to get. I pulled out of the parking lot and made my way toward the freeway in silence.

Charlie had somehow managed to forgive me by the time his birthday rolled around that weekend. The morning of his party he seemed unfazed by the sweater and jeans I laid out for him to wear to Jump Around. I was surprised he didn't try to argue for a more feminine ensemble. *Off to a great start*, I thought to myself as we left our house, my stomach still twisted in knots with anticipatory anxiety.

The kids all jumped around and climbed the structures. That is, until "Let it Go" was piped through the speakers halfway through playtime.

My fight-or-flight anxiety kicked in. I quickly scanned the area for Charlie. There he was, dancing around the enclosed trampoline with his arms outstretched. I let out a small chuckle when I saw him and then let my eyes dart around the room. Some of the other kids had stopped what they were doing on the equipment and were singing and dancing to the song in their own way too. They were spellbound. It was like the song had hypnotized them.

No harm done, I thought. Charlie was not behaving any differently than most of the other kids. I could relax again.

One of the things that had been awkward for me in planning the party was the cake. Charlie had wanted an "Elsa" cake, but it was a hit for everyone, and if any adult thought it was weird that my little boy had a cake with Elsa from *Frozen* on it, they didn't show it. Charlie sat grinning ear to ear, perched atop a huge plastic throne with a gold paper crown on his head as we sang Happy Birthday. He looked super cute, even if I knew he felt more like a princess than like a king. Charlie was happy, and I had made it through the party without embarrassment.

A week after Charlie's birthday celebration, I wanted to finally reach out to the family of a little girl Charlie was starting to bond with at school. Mandy had mentioned at pick-up one day that Charlie was often holding hands with a couple of the girls in his class during story time.

When I asked him about it, his eyes lit up and he replied, "Mom! I really like Sophia. She is my friend! Can we have a playdate?"

I was already ahead of him.

"Well, honey," I responded, "I think we certainly could. Let me reach out to her mom."

While I was nervous to introduce my gender-bending child to another family, I also knew that I needed to foster whatever positive relationships Charlie had, but I had no idea what sort of values or beliefs Sophia's family adhered to, and I needed to make sure that they would be accepting and understanding of whatever identity Charlie chose to present to them. I decided to write an email to Sophia's mother.

Dear Victoria, I began the email. *My name is Tasha, and I'm Charlie's mom from preschool. I hear from Mandy that Sophia and Charlie are holding hands frequently during story time.*

I paused then, thinking about what I wanted to tell her next. Should I write, "I'm the mom with the gender-fluid kid?" or, "My son might look like a girl, but…" No, not that way, I chastised myself. I wanted to be honest, but couldn't I also be graceful in my approach? I continued with, *I wanted to ask you if you would allow Sophia to have a playdate with Charlie sometime? I do, however, want to be honest about something. Charlie has been telling us for a while now that he is a girl. We are not sure what it means fully, but I just wanted to let you know in case Sophia has told you anything she has heard at school.*

I asked her to let me know if she wanted to schedule a date and then I quickly clicked the send button before I could change my mind. As I pushed back from the dining room table, I could feel my palms had turned sweaty. I had to look away from the computer; otherwise, I would drive myself crazy waiting for a response to come through. *Give her some time to respond*, I told myself. *Relax*. But I was far from relaxed.

I distracted myself by making a sandwich in the kitchen, and after fifteen minutes, I couldn't take it anymore. As I sat down in front of the screen, sure enough, I could see a new email had come through from Victoria. I held my breath as I clicked on the email.

Hi Tasha, it began, *Thanks for reaching out about a play date. I have heard that Sophia and Charlie are getting along quite well at school, and it's super cute that they are holding hands! We would love to get together sometime! Thanks for sharing about Charlie—we felt like he was a pretty feminine little boy, so we are not surprised! But this does not bother us in the least! Let's get together at the park maybe? How does a couple of Saturdays from now look to you?*

I breathed a sigh of relief as I wrote back.

A few days later, Charlie approached me with a serious look on his face. "Mommy, tomorrow I want to wear a dress to my school," he said. His eyes were pleading but his voice remained calm.

Oh, god. Here we go.

Even though I had a feeling this day would come, I still was not prepared at all. I could tell by looking at him that Charlie would not take no for an answer, so there was no use in arguing. I could feel myself becoming light-headed. I knelt down next to him, as much to steady myself as to be on his level. I took a deep breath and tried to keep the anxiety out of my voice.

"You want to wear a dress, honey?" I said, trying to smile.

"Yes, I do," he nodded. "Help me pick one out!"

He was so absolute in his resolve. It was something I admired about him. When he made up his mind, that was it. My mind flashed back to the days when I was in high school, walking to my locker in MC Hammer parachute pants.

I said yes. Then, I followed him up the stairs to go through the handful of dresses we had recently accumulated for him. With the biggest smile on his face, he chose a blue one with a yellow ribbon around the waist. I should have been happy to see my child so excited—it was such a pretty dress after all—but I felt nothing but dread.

It felt as though I were sinking in quicksand, and unable to claw my way to the surface. I managed to smile back at Charlie but couldn't speak, for fear I would cry. I knew right then and there that I would not be able to be the one to take him to school in the dress. I didn't have the strength yet. Brian would have to do it.

I raised the situation with Brian over dinner that night.

"S-so," I stammered as I thought about the words I wanted to use. "Charlie wants to wear a dress to school tomorrow. We already picked one out together. I just can't do it. I need you to take him."

I was talking fast, trying to get it all out there before I lost my nerve to say it.

"I just—I don't feel brave enough to face everyone. I think I might start crying if someone gave me—or Charlie for that matter—a disapproving look or something. I couldn't take it. Will you take him?" I said this last part with hopeful trepidation. What if Brian couldn't do it either?

He didn't answer right away. I knew he saw the fear I was feeling inside.

When he finally spoke, he said, "Yes, I'll take him."

He said it quietly but matter-of-factly. He might not have felt brave enough either, but he could see that I needed his help, and so did Charlie.

All I could think about as I lay in bed that night was Charlie wearing a dress to school and everyone laughing at him. It would be devastating, for him and for me. Even though I had emailed his teacher, Mandy, and she was on board to help him with any situation he might encounter—especially negative —I was still anxiety-ridden. I knew wearing a dress would make Charlie happy, but all I could think of was impending doom. It was a long sleepless night.

The next morning came like a freight train, barreling fast and furiously through my consciousness. I was no more ready to face the situation at hand than I had been the night before, and I wasn't even the one taking him to school! I feigned a smile for Charlie when he twirled for me in his new blue dress before getting into the car.

"You look so pretty," I said, choking back the tears.

I leaned into the open window of the car to kiss Brian and say goodbye. I reached out to stroke his face and said, "I love you, honey. Thank you." He nodded solemnly at me, his eyes watery as he rolled up the window and drove away.

I was on pins and needles the entire time Brian was gone. It felt like an eternity waiting for him to return from school. As soon as he pulled into the drive, I scurried out the front door to receive the full report. I wanted to get it over with. I must have been like a hurricane hurtling towards him, but Brian stayed calm as I approached the car. He held out his arms and enveloped me in a big bear hug. I let him hug me, then pulled away and immediately started talking.

"So, what happened? Is Charlie okay? How did it all go with Mandy? Was she nice? Was everyone nice? Did anyone say anything mean? Please tell me no one was mean." The words kept gushing out of me, even as I tried to hold them back.

Brian paused to close the door of the car. As he turned towards me, he grabbed my hands in his and said, "It was fine. Everything was fine. Nothing bad happened at all. Mandy was great."

I was still anxious, not sure I believed him that everything had been fine.

"I wasn't feeling all that brave this morning, either. I was nervous to walk him in and face all those parents. But actually, it was Sophia's dad Lance who was the first parent we saw when Charlie and I walked up to the school, and he said, 'That's a nice dress, Charlie.' It was not what I expected—from anyone."

I could tell Brian was getting choked up. He took a moment, then continued quietly.

"That gave me some strength to walk him all the way into the classroom."

After he finished the story, I just stared at him. Had Victoria told her husband what I had said to her about Charlie? I wasn't sure, but whether she had or not didn't matter. He had unknowingly helped my husband through one of the most difficult moments of fatherhood. I knew Brian would be forever grateful. It could have so easily gone another way.

Charlie began to wear dresses to school fairly frequently after that.

I was so grateful that the experience had been such a positive one. I was proud of how the preschool had reacted and had worked to make sure he was comfortable.

I should have felt validated by the decision Brian and I had made to let him wear a dress and also by the positive reactions he received, but, amazingly enough, I didn't feel validated at all. I felt ever more alone and afraid. I wasn't able to control what happened to Charlie, and I felt crushed under the weight of what I assumed the future would bring. Just because Charlie had a positive experience at this school did not mean he would get the same acceptance in other places. After all, there were all kinds of different people in the world with all kinds of different viewpoints.

Besides Brian, and to some extent my parents, no one really knew the level of my fear and anxiety. We had told our friends that Charlie was more and more identifying as a female, but we were not opening up to them about the emotional toll it was taking on us. I was worried—all the time—and could not see how to get it under control.

As Christmas loomed closer, the anxiety was excruciating. I was not a person who normally had bouts of depression, but I was starting to understand that was exactly the darkness I was beginning to fall into. *I don't know if I have the strength to do this,* I often said to myself. *Maybe it would be better—even for Charlie—if I just died. I don't know if I'm strong enough to help him.*

The thoughts of death were overwhelming. I had no intention of killing myself, but sometimes I thought, *Well, if I get sick and die, maybe it's for the best. I'm not sure I'm equipped to handle this.*

I finally revealed my dark secret to Brian one night after the kids were in bed.

"I sometimes feel like it might be easier if I just died," I said quietly as we sat together on the couch, the TV off.

Brian's eyes got very wide.

"What?! Honey, that's crazy. Don't talk like that. I can't believe you just said that!"

He wasn't yelling at me; he was more flabbergasted than anything.

"I'm not going to kill myself or anything, babe. I just mean that I don't know if I have the strength for all that this will entail for him in his life—if this goes where it seems to be going. What if I'm hindering him with my weakness? That's why I feel like if I just wasn't here anymore, it might be better."

I knew it didn't make sense and that I sounded deranged and illogical. Brian was careful not to insult me. He waited a minute before responding.

"That's ridiculous, honey. Charlie needs you; we all need you, but I'm your partner. You are not alone in this. We are in this together. You are stronger than you know. We will get through this however we have to."

He looked at me. He was mostly right. I probably was stronger than I knew, but boy, was that being tested! I would have to dig deep to find that strength, for us and for both my children.

Until Brian said it out loud, I had almost forgotten that I was not all alone. Sometimes it was so easy to feel suffocated by the anxiety and fear that I forgot that I had a partner going through the same exact situation, holding my hand. *Thank god for my husband,* I told myself, n*ow more than ever.*

I was still pretty down in the dumps as the holidays approached. Usually, I was super excited for everything that the season had to offer—presents, decorations, decadent desserts, and lots of festive get-togethers with friends. Not this year. I felt dread on an almost daily basis.

I was at a fairly low point when I received a text from one of our dear friends. Nina was inviting us over for an ugly holiday sweater-themed party. It would be a small group, just six families. Our kids were expected to be there. I felt the pit in my stomach grow bigger as I read the last part of the text.

Our kids are expected to be there. Ugh. I was in no mood to field questions about Charlie. I had no energy whatsoever to discuss the details of what we were all going through. I was depressed, fearful, and somewhat angry. I was like a boat lost at sea in the dark. I knew Brian was trying to help guide me back to the light, but right now I wasn't in a place to accept his help.

If only this were a Halloween party, I could at least hide most of my emotions under some sort of costume. I could pretend we were all completely different people and that none of this was happening. It would be so much easier to bring Charlie to the party in a dress that way. It would be his unique costume—nothing more! If only things were that easy.

The day of the party, we were going through the many boxes of Christmas decorations that we had acquired over the years when Charlie came upon a Santa hat. *Not again,* I thought, remembering how he had worn one nonstop to mimic long hair the previous year. Of course, this was the hat he wanted to wear to the ugly sweater party. How could I say no? It was a Christmas-themed event.

There were only going to be my very best friends at the party. That should have made me feel more comfortable. But it didn't. I wouldn't care much about what a bunch of strangers thought of my child. I'd likely never see them again. I knew our friends loved us—I just couldn't deal with all the questions and the potential that I might see pity in their eyes. A look of pity would gut me. I didn't want anyone to feel sorry for us. I would feel pathetic and damaged. My very social husband really wanted to go, however, so I had to find a way to rally. I took a couple deep breaths and exhaled before I pulled the ugliest holiday sweater I'd ever owned over my head. For the first time in my life, I couldn't wait for this party to be over.

"Mommy?" Charlie said on the way to the party, "you and daddy need to call me Room on the Broom today at the party. I'm not Charlie. See my hair?"

He whipped his head back and forth, swinging the long-tapered end of the Santa hat as if it were a long ponytail.

Oh god, I thought. He hadn't been Room on the Broom for months. He had been any number of other characters—including Elsa from *Frozen* almost exclusively, so I thought this one had effectively been put to rest.

But it wasn't a request. It was a demand.

Brian kept his eyes trained to the road and shrugged, as if to say, "Oh, well. Just do it."

This was my worst fear imagined. How embarrassing. The last thing I needed was for our friends to think our kid was weird. I wanted our children to stand out for their talents and abilities, not because they had strange proclivities and were misunderstood. I was hoping to not have to talk much at the party about what we were going through with Charlie and his gender identity. Now it seemed, I would have to. I could feel the anxiety brewing inside of me. I wanted to turn the car around and skip the party altogether, but we were already on our way. I could not turn back now and risk having to answer our friends—or Charlie—about why we didn't go.

I was a bundle of nerves as we walked into Nina's house. I was still trying to devise a way to avoid having to call my child Room on the Broom for the next several hours. I hadn't figured it out yet. As we crossed the threshold, we saw our good friends Cara and Alex and Erin and Justin. I made eye contact with my friend Jenny across the room, and she gave me a beaming smile. I knew we had a lot of catching up to do. I hugged my friends that were gathered around the front door and then saw that Cara's mom, Shay, had come to the party as well.

"Charlie, honey, this is Cara's mom, Shay," I said as I pulled away from our embrace to reintroduce her to my child. He was already playing with some blocks on the living room floor but stopped quickly to admonish me in front of Shay.

"Mom, I'm Room on the Broom," Charlie said with conviction. I tried to smile while a bit of nervous laughter escaped my mouth.

"Okay, honey. Whatever."

Shay eyed me with a curious look and laughed nervously. I felt the need to further explain. "He loves this character from a book. She's a witch. Room on the Broom," I mustered. "He's into playing different characters these days. This one has a long braid, and that hat is supposed to be her hair," I finished the explanation, though I felt like I had said much more than I had needed to. Shay had three grown children. She knew kids did lots of pretending, didn't she?

As Shay moved to the door to greet more people, I walked swiftly to the kitchen and poured myself a very stiff cocktail.

As the party wore on, I began to care less and less about the impression Room on the Broom was making at the party as the booze started to take effect. *Don't get too blitzed,* I thought to myself, *stay on the buzzed path.* I looked over at Oliver and could see he was bouncing back and forth between a couple of my girlfriends, grinning ear to ear and enjoying the attention. He was already a ladies' man at just one year old. I looked over the railing of the back patio and could see Brian in the backyard chatting with the guys. A couple of them were making big gestures with their hands and laughing hysterically. My family all looked happy and accounted for—except for Room on the Broom. Where was he?

I searched the entire main floor first. I found a couple of kids playing trucks in the living room, one of the older boys begging for food in the kitchen, and when I knocked on the bathroom door, it was not Charlie's voice that hollered back. Nina's girls both had rooms downstairs, so I descended the stairs to check for him there.

On the staircase, I looked to my right and immediately saw Charlie. He did not see me—and right away I realized that I did not want him to. I sat down silently on a step so I could quietly observe him. He was wearing a pink princess dress and moving slowly, gracefully, around the playroom. His movement was similar to a butterfly, something between dancing and fluttering. As I sat there watching my child, my friend Jenny started to come down the stairs to look for her girls. She knew in an instant not to continue down the stairs past me. Jenny sat down and we exchanged the knowing looks that mothers sometimes do, and we watched Charlie together. As he kept dancing in the chiffon dress, soon I could tell that he had something in his hands. When he twirled around, I could finally see what it was: A doll.

A Barbie doll, to be exact, with long blonde hair and a pink dress. I smiled nervously at Jenny. She reached over and gently rubbed my back with her hand. Oddly enough I felt comforted by the gesture rather than embarrassed. We continued to watch Charlie together as he danced around the room with the Barbie. Then, ever so slowly, he lifted Barbie over his head and casually looked under her dress. My heart leapt into my throat, and for a moment, I was paralyzed.

"Holy shit, what just happened?" I whispered to Jenny as soon as I gained some composure.

Jenny kept her gaze on Charlie as she answered me.

"He wanted to see what parts she has. The doll. He's curious about her parts."

Instead of being disgusted or confused, Jenny seemed impressed. She looked at me and continued her thoughts.

"He's trying to figure it out. The doll has a dress on and long hair. Do the doll's private parts match how she is displaying herself to the world? Or could she have boy parts under there?" Jenny's eyes bore into mine. I knew what she really meant.

My friends knew more about what was going on with Charlie than I had ever ventured to consider.

"Wow. He looked at what parts she has? Holy shit. What do you think he thought when he looked? Disappointment?" I was asking Jenny, but I was really asking myself.

"Well," she finally said, "Maybe. Or maybe this is helping him figure out that he can have boy parts and look like a girl at the same time, and that is okay. Eventually, he will look to you and Brian to make sure however he feels is validated," she said, squeezing my hand.

You've got this, the squeeze said.

I felt as though I was trying to swim with all my clothes on and was being pulled under the water.

"What do I do?" I asked her with desperation, like Jenny could save me from drowning. She was one of the most spiritual people I knew, and her answer was all I needed to hear in that moment.

"I think you are already doing great. You are loving him no matter what. This is something bigger than us all. I think, maybe, his spirit *chose* you and Brian. He chose you to be his parents," Jenny paused, just long enough for me to realize I was holding my breath. "So," she persisted, "you'll figure it out as you go."

It was a moving proclamation. I swallowed hard and gave her a feeble smile. "God, I hope you are right."

It took me some time to fully process what I had seen and what Jenny had said. It was a few days before I told Brian. When I did, he was overcome with emotion.

"Wow Tash. Oh my god. He wanted to see the doll's parts. He must be so confused," he said, as he wiped tears from his eyes. Brian's empathy was one of the reasons I loved him.

"He must feel like his inside doesn't match his outside. How horrible," I replied.

Brian gathered himself suddenly and said, "But what Jenny said—about Charlie choosing us—I mean, that's amazing. I believe that. He was meant to be our child; I know that in my bones."

"Yes," I replied without hesitation. I knew it was true too. I was not a religious person, but I did believe in the human spirit, in energy—maybe even fate. "He—or she, whichever it is—this child is magical. Special. Ours."

Now I was the emotional one.

"It's our job to be there for him, protect him, help him, whatever we can," Brian said. "This is confusing, and we don't have all the answers, but we have to stop thinking about ourselves and think about him, what he needs."

He was impassioned, talking quickly, full of love. It was like a lightbulb went on.

"Basically, we just need to get over our shit," I said.

"Yes. We need to get over our own shit. We need to stop worrying about what everyone else thinks, feels, knows, and just *be there* for our child. Accept him—or her. We need to worry only about Charlie."

At that moment, the depression I had felt over the last month completely melted away. I was still going to be scared, confused, and probably angry at times.

But now I also knew that no matter what, I would be there for my child.

CHAPTER TWELVE

Charlie was absolutely ecstatic to go to the show, so I wasn't super surprised when he bounded down the stairs in his Elsa dress right as we were about to leave to go see Disney's Frozen on Ice.

"Mom! I'm wearing my Elsa dress to Frozen on Ice! I'm Elsa!" He twirled around and flicked his longish hair side to side, like any diva would.

I had to stifle my giggle. I didn't want him to think I was laughing at him. The truth was, he was the cutest little Elsa I had ever seen! I wasn't so sure people at the show would think the same. Would they know he was a boy? We were about to find out. Baby steps, I told myself. If anyone said anything to us, or him—God forbid—I would tell them to go to hell. Don't mess with Mama Bear!

Frozen on Ice was everything Charlie wanted and more. He got his picture taken with his newly acquired Elsa doll and the photographer even referred to him as a girl—and I did not correct him. Charlie got a huge tub of popcorn and M&Ms all to himself. I watched his little face change when the Elsa character skated onto the rink. He lit up from the inside out. *This isn't so bad*, I thought to myself. I could do this. No one even blinked an eye in his direction, let alone made a comment. Maybe people were more accepting than I thought—or maybe he could pass as a girl. Whatever the case, we had made it through. No ugly confrontations or evil looks, and I had kept myself from growing overly nervous and trying to control everything. What a success!

Fail, succeed, fail again. Then another success. *I am human*, I told myself. *All I can do is keep trying, for me and for Charlie.*

Charlie seemed to be turning into my little girl more and more with each passing day. He preferred to wear dresses almost all the time at home and he asked that we refer to him by the name Elsa rather than Charlie. We were actually beginning to get used to the whole routine.

One day Charlie came up behind me after I got home from work and wrapped his little arms around my waist. I knew my baby needed me for something. After I hugged him back for a minute or two, I unwrapped his arms from my sides and bent down to be on eye level with him. As soon as he had my attention, he launched in.

"Mom. I want to be Elsa when I'm at my school too and always wear my dresses," he paused, trying to feel me out. "I'm a girl, so I don't want to be Charlie at school anymore." His big brown eyes shined with the seriousness of a much older person. I had to remind myself that he had just turned four.

"Oh, honey," I started very carefully, "I know you probably do, but they know you as Charlie. It might confuse all the kids if you change your name at school. You can still wear dresses at school sometimes, but let's just wait on the other stuff for now."

By "other stuff," I meant everything else in Pandora's box of gender confusion. I was trying to keep the lid halfway on as long as I could.

His face showed the disappointment that I knew he felt in his heart. I tried to soothe him.

"You know we call you Elsa here at home. That's fine with us. We love you! You are beautiful!" I hugged him tight to me and prayed that his desires were satiated enough to keep this recent request at bay for a while longer.

"Okay," he said.

He said it with a sadness in his voice that cut through my heart like a sharp blade. As he skulked off to watch TV, I had to choke back sobs.

After putting Charlie to bed that night, I found Brian in his office.

"We have to talk," I said.

He already knew it had to be about Charlie—that's what most of our serious conversations were about these days.

Brian looked at me warily.

"Yes, honey? What's up?" His voice was calm but his face revealed his concern.

I crumpled into his arms, and the tears poured down my face. Between sobs, I managed to explain the current situation.

"Charlie told me tonight that he wants to be a girl all the time, including at school," I stopped wailing long enough to let the seriousness of my words sink in for Brian. We locked eyes, and I continued. "This can't happen right now. I mean, I'm not ready! We need to wait until the next school year if this is how it is going to be. How can we do this now?" I was exasperated and couldn't make myself calm. Brian grabbed my hands in his.

"I am not sure. I don't know what to say. I want Charlie to be happy. I know he says he wants this, but we are his parents. He doesn't know all the other ins and outs associated with a decision like this. We are supposed to protect him." Brian was usually logical, and this situation was shaping up to not be any different.

I was nodding now, and my sobbing was under control. "Yes, I agree. He's barely four. He can't know the consequences of a decision like this. We have to think of all of that and protect him," I paused for a second to think. "I just want him—her—whatever—to be happy. Can we make sure our child is happy, even though we are not listening to his needs?"

I was skeptical but also needed to be right. I could not fathom 'transitioning' my child to live publicly as the opposite gender—at least not yet. I had said to myself before that I needed to get over my own personal fears so that my child could truly be happy.

But I was beginning to see that living that truth was not as easy as saying it.

I knew at this point that we really should talk to some other parents of transgender and gender-fluid kids. I, at least, needed to feel some support from other families who could relate to what we were going through. I remembered that Darlene, the therapist we had seen a couple of times, had mentioned a support group of sorts, made up of other families like ours. I emailed her to ask about the local support group.

Hi Darlene, I wrote, *Charlie is really starting to present as a girl to us more and more. He wants to be a girl at school!!!* I used three exclamation marks for extreme emphasis so Darlene would know my intense concern. *Can I please have the contact for the gender identity (or is it transgender??) support group you told us about a while back? We need to talk to some other parents.*

I pushed the send button as I choked back tears. Maybe we would meet these other families and realize that Charlie wasn't anything like those kids. Maybe it really was a phase, but I knew as I thought the thought that it was so far out of bounds. We were way past that possibility. I knew ultimately we were going to meet parents that had children just like Charlie, and that hopefully they could help guide us through the next steps. At the very least, they could reassure us that everything was going to be okay.

Darlene wrote back half an hour later. *Hi! Good to hear from you. Here is the location for the support group. They meet every first Sunday of the month. It is so great. And don't worry, everything is going to be okay. Let me know if you want to do a session again soon! Take care! - Darlene.*

I grabbed a pen and wrote down the address.

The meeting was in four days.

On the day of the support group meeting, I was a bundle of nerves. On one hand, I was ready to be surrounded by other parents that could relate to the concerns and fears that we had for our gender-fluid child. On the other hand, I was very anxious that they would give me more information than I was ready to hear. But I knew I couldn't have it both ways. I had to trust that we were doing the right thing at the right time.

The meeting was held in a church. I reminded myself that Charlie's preschool was affiliated with a church and had so far done all the right things. *I must trust the universe,* I told myself, as we entered the church.

The main meeting room was filled with at least thirty adults. Some in the group arrived with children in tow, but the children stayed outside to play on the playground so the parents could chat without worrying about their children listening in. It was good to know that in the future we could bring our kids to a meeting—that is, if we decided that we would come back.

Tom, the organizer of the support group, announced to everyone in the room that he would be dividing the group up according to their children's ages. We split into two groups, one for parents with children under ten years old and another group for parents whose children were over ten.

Thank god, I thought to myself. I didn't need to hear about puberty and teenage bullying now—I wouldn't be able to handle it!

Brian and I walked to the back of the church to find the assigned room for our meeting. I had no idea what to expect as we pushed open the door. I had already planned to mostly just sit and listen. If I could find a seat in the back of the room, that would be great. As we walked in, I could see that my plan was not going to work out. Unfortunately, the room was set up with about twenty chairs formed together in a circle in the middle of the room.

Oh great, I thought. I couldn't hide in the back after all. Brian and I exchanged wary glances and sat down in two chairs by the windows. As everyone filtered in, I began to relax. *These are my people,* I told myself. I didn't know any of them yet, but I already felt a sense of calm wash over me as I thought about how I could already relate to these complete strangers.

We went around the circle and introduced ourselves and gave some background information about our children. Some of the parents were short and to the point with their information. It was evident that these parents had been coming to this group meeting for some time. They required no assurances from the rest of us. From what I could tell, they were there to reassure the rest of us—the "newbies."

When the new parents spoke, it was generally at great length. A lot of people asked questions about what was normal and what they should do to help their child. There were a couple mothers who had come to the group alone. The fathers were not accepting of their children's identities and, therefore, didn't see the need to bare their souls to a group of strangers. I felt so much empathy for these women, as I couldn't imagine what it would be like if I didn't have Brian to help me through this experience.

When it was our turn, I glanced at Brian. The look on his face told me to speak for us.

"Hi everyone," I began nervously. "My name is Tasha and this is my husband Brian. We have a son that is four, and he's been telling us since he was about two years old that he is a girl. It has gotten more frequent and intense in the last year or so."

I looked awkwardly at Brian, pleading with my eyes for him to interject.

"We don't know if it is a phase or not," he said. "He has been so consistent, so we don't really think so anymore, but we are still confused." I could see he was starting to get choked up as he tried to continue. "It's just, you know, we love him so much." He had to pause as tears filled his eyes.

I waited for him to say more, but it was clear that if he kept talking, he would start crying in front of these strangers. I knew I had to take over again.

"I guess we are here because we just don't know what to do. Did you all have this type of experience? We want to do the right thing by Charlie. We want him to be happy, but we don't want to jump the gun on anything either." I looked around the room, hoping that someone would just tell us what to do.

There was a collective pause amongst the group. Then a woman on my left with long brown hair began to speak.

"Hi Brian, hi Tasha. My name is Christy. We have an eight-year-old transgender daughter named Jessie." I could tell she was one of the leaders of the group, and I looked to her as a person of authority with regards to navigating a gender-fluid child's journey.

"Hi," I said, somewhat tersely, as I was already on the defensive, even though I had no idea what Christy was going to say.

"So," Christy continued, "you need to transition her."

She used the feminine pronoun when referring to my son—whom she didn't even know—and this really irked me.

"I'm sorry, what?" The words just flew out of my mouth. "So soon?"

"How do you know we shouldn't wait?" Brian chimed in, his emotions under control.

Christy was calm but deliberate in her response. "I know this is hard to process. Most of us have been there," her eyes darted around the room and several people nodded their heads in agreement. "I don't know your child, but I do know that the sooner you transition her, the better—for her." She stared at me as she said this, and I could see warmth and care in her eyes.

After a long pause, I found my voice.

"Can't we wait until the new school year? Next September? That would be so much easier."

Christy was resolute in her response.

"That might be what is best for you guys," she said. "But it would actually be better for her to transition now."

I knew she had a transgender daughter herself, but I was still unconvinced that she knew what was best for my child, my family. I didn't want to become defensive, especially with a group of strangers trying to help us.

"I'm not sure," I finally said. "We have to think."

Christy seemed to know that we were done discussing Charlie, and the room moved to discuss other parents' concerns. After another twenty minutes of discussion, the meeting was over, and we all stood to file out of the room.

As we were walking out into the courtyard, I saw her. Hillary. The woman from the YouTube video! The video that had opened my eyes to the possibility that I might have a transgender child back when Charlie was two and a half. I couldn't believe this. Before I lost my nerve, I blurted out, "Hillary? Are you from that video on YouTube, with your son?"

Hillary's face lit up with a smile.

"Yes, that's me. My son is Ryland."

Without even thinking I leaned into her with my arms out to hug her. Even though I was a stranger, she could tell that I needed comfort from her, so she wrapped her arms around me and held on.

As I pulled away from the embrace, I said, "Thank you."

"Yes. I know how you feel. It's going to be okay. You can call me whenever you want to talk," Hillary said, tears in her eyes.

We exchanged phone numbers before saying our goodbyes.

As Brian and I walked to our car, everything we'd just experienced started to sink in. Meeting Hillary had been the most reassuring thing to come from the meeting, even more so than the advice we had heard from the group. I found out later from her that that was the first meeting she and her husband had been to in almost a year.

In the week following the group meeting, Brian and I discussed the advice we had been given by the parents. Though they were complete strangers, they were going through— or had gone through—a lot of the same challenges we were. Most of their feelings and experiences mirrored ours.

A few nights later, Brian turned to me and said, "Gosh, that parent meeting was great. The most important thing is that we are not alone. I can't believe I got emotional. I mean, it's an emotional situation, you know? But I can't believe how easily it came in front of those strangers." He looked a little sheepish, and I put my hand on top of his.

"Oh, love, you love your child. That was abundantly clear. Did you see how a lot of those men took the longest time accepting that their child is transgender? Especially if their child was their firstborn son. But you, you may have been confused, like me, but you always accepted him —her," I stammered. "There was no shaming from the father. That's huge. Shame does something awful to a person's psyche."

I drifted off then, the weight of everything we had learned and everything I had just said sinking in.

I was reassured to know other parents that had similar obstacles to overcome, similar situations to compare between our children. At the same time, a lot of what they had said to us also scared the crap out of me. My gut told me my child was transgender, but my head told me to hold off with the official transition, at least until the new school year.

I began speaking again, with all the conviction that I could muster. "I just don't agree with them on the transition." My eyes met Brian's gaze and locked. "At least, not yet."

Brian raised his eyebrows.

"You agree that he *should* transition, just not now?" He skipped along with his thoughts before I even had a chance to respond. "I think we should wait until at least the next school year."

"Oh, honey, I agree!" I felt relieved I didn't have to explain my thought process to him, though I proceeded to launch into the reasons why anyway, probably just to reassure myself. "I mean, he's not even four and a half! What difference will six months make? I'll explain it to him; he will understand. It would be so much easier to start a new class at school as a female—rather than changing halfway through the year. How hard would that be?" I was talking fast again, something I did often when I was anxious.

Brian was easily convinced. He didn't look forward to the transition and what it entailed any more than I did. "I totally agree. Next September makes the most sense."

Brian nodded at me and that was that. We both felt good. We had a plan.

A couple weeks later, I was putting groceries away in the kitchen when Charlie bounded into the room after he and Brian returned from preschool. He looked ecstatic. He was wearing a green floral dress we had just picked up at Target.

"Hi baby. How was school today?" I began the conversation, waiting for him to tell me about a game they played or a new book that Miss Mandy read at circle time.

"It was good, Mommy," he paused, filling his pink plastic cup with water. "Um, so I told everyone at school today that I'm really a girl and that my name is now Elsa."

He said it matter-of-factly, like he was telling me he liked wheat bread rather than white.

I was so caught off guard, I dropped the tomato I had in my hand. It fell to the hardwood floor with a splat. Tomato juice oozed out onto the floor, spattering onto my new cream-colored shoes.

"Damn," I said under my breath. Charlie's (Elsa's?) eyes flickered with concern. I didn't want him to think that I was angry with him about the news he had shared with me.

"My shoes! Crap! I can't believe I did that," I quickly exclaimed, my hand shaking as I bent over to pick up the remains of the tomato from the floor.

"Oh no, Mom, sorry!" His face softened as he took a drink of his water and walked out of the kitchen.

Crisis avoided, I thought to myself, but I was a bundle of nerves inside. Now the plan Brian and I had made was completely shot to hell. I looked to Brian, who had entered the room just in time to hear everything. His eyes were wide as saucers, but he remained silent.

"Oh, my god. I think our child just transitioned, er, herself," I consciously changed the pronoun, knowing now that it was permanent, whether I was ready or not.

Brian and I discussed the transition—and the fact that we now had a daughter—that night after both kids were in bed. She made it abundantly clear to us that we were on her timeline, not our own.

"It's not all that surprising," I said to Brian after taking a large swig of my red wine. "I mean, that she just did it her own way." He looked at me and said, "No, it's not. We were fools to believe we could hold off the transition until September."

"She knew we were reticent. Amazing. The courage that child has—it's so inspiring."

My eyes welled up with tears. It had all happened the way that it was supposed to. Like Jenny had said to me before—this child chose us as parents. That's when I realized that Charlie had really been Elsa all along. She'd been patiently leading us—Brian, my parents, and myself—to this truth that she already knew in her heart and soul. She was *our* teacher, rather than the other way around.

In following my child's lead, I found acceptance.

CHAPTER THIRTEEN

After everything we had been through together as a family, I concluded that we all needed a trip to the happiest place on earth, so I booked a trip to Disneyland.

When I booked the trip for us, Elsa was still Charlie. She had not transitioned yet. But as the day approached, I realized that I would be planning an excursion for a little girl rather than a little boy.

Our former nanny Margarita was still very close to our family, she had practically helped us to raise Elsa until she was two years old. She was also a Disneyland expert. She went to the park on a monthly basis and knew how to cram all the most fun rides and activities into a two-day adventure. One night after she watched the kids, I asked her what we should put on our "to-do" list.

"Oh my god!" she squealed. "You have to take her to the Bippity Boppity Boutique!"

"What is the...Bippity Boppity Boutique?" I asked.

"Oh, it is so much fun," she said. "The girls get to dress as whatever princess they want, and then they get their hair and makeup done too. They are totally transformed into Disney princesses!"

It all sounded great to me. My son had become my daughter and was starting to transform how the world would see her and know her as a person both inside and out. How appropriate to have her experience a physical transformation that would, in a sense, mirror the truth she was feeling on the inside. I immediately went onto the website to book her appointment. I wanted her to have a truly girly experience, so I chose a package that included a dress, makeup, and hair. It was not cheap.

I was so excited to tell Elsa about the appointment I had booked at the Boutique. When I told her that night, she gave me the reaction I had expected.

"Oh, Mommy, I get to be Elsa for real!" she screamed while dancing around our living room.

My heart was full of love for her, but then her response sank in a bit. I didn't want her to think that she had to be a Disney princess to live life as a girl. I wanted her to know that she could just be herself.

"Honey, you already are the real Elsa, but yes, they will make you look exactly like the Elsa from the movie." I gave her a big grin, and she smiled back, throwing her arms around my neck in a big hug.

"Yay, Mommy, I'm so excited!"

I was excited too because I had made her happy with this plan. She would get to present to the world, not just as her favorite character in a movie like every other girl at the Boutique, but also as the gender she truly believed herself to be.

For the first time in my life, I couldn't wait to go to Disneyland.

We arrived at the Bippity Boppity Boutique just before our one p.m. appointment, and the place was a madhouse. Girls of all ages packed the store. Some were already wearing the Disney princess dress of their choice, while others gathered around the racks of dresses trying to decide which princess they wanted to become for the day. There were dozens of dresses, shoes, tiaras, sashes, wands, headbands, socks, hats, capes, jewelry, and other accessories, from floor to ceiling, all pertaining to any Disney princess you could imagine. A girl could transform into Rapunzel, Snow White, or Merida from *Brave*, for instance, and find all the accouterments in this store to complete the ensemble.

Honestly, I just wanted to run out of the store screaming. There were so many people, and it was just so, well, girly. It was obsessive in nature, really, but I put all of those thoughts out of my head because at that moment, it was about making my daughter happy. She couldn't have been more excited to be there and ran around the store touching every dress she could reach, shouting to me as she did this.

"Mommy, look! It's Mulan's dress! Mommy, wait, look at the Rapunzel braid! I want long hair, Mommy! Mommy! It's Aurora! I want this dress!" She went on like this until she found the Elsa dress in the corner.

"Oh…Mommy! It's a new Elsa dress! I want this one, Mommy!" She said this so loudly that in normal circumstances everyone in the store would have turned around to look at us, but since it was so incredibly busy in there, her request blended in with all the other girls screaming out their excitement. She had almost worn out the Elsa dress she already had, and this one was much fancier.

I grabbed the Elsa dress in her size and guided her to the back of the room where the appointments were fulfilled. We approached what appeared to be a hostess desk, with a woman wearing what could only be a fairy godmother costume (and way too much eye makeup).

"Hello dear, do you have an appointment with us today?" the woman asked me.

"Yes, for my daughter at one p.m.," I responded.

"Oh great, she grinned, what is her name?"

"Her name is Elsa," I said, with conviction. I wondered if she would take us seriously.

"Oh, isn't that great! I bet she was over the moon when she saw *Frozen* and realized that the princess had her same name!"

Little did she know that my child chose her own name after watching the movie, but this was not the time—nor the place—for explanations.

"Yes, that's right," I said with a smile.

I walked her back to the dressing room and helped her change into the Elsa dress. Afterwards, the hostess proceeded to lead us back out into the room that was lined with salon chairs. She put Elsa into a chair against the wall, flanked by girls of various ages getting their makeovers. We were then introduced to our very own "fairy godmother" who would be the stylist for our makeover.

We chose a hairstyle from three selections that were pictured on a laminated card. Her hair would be swept up into a bun, with a trail of long hair (which was a wig) falling down the length of her back. Elsa had always been obsessed with long hair, so this seemed to fit her perfectly. I was so excited for her.

The fairy godmother began repeatedly combing and spraying her hair, sometimes with regular hairspray and other times with something that involved glitter. As this routine continued, Elsa began to look around her at the other girls seated in chairs next to her on either side and across from her. They too were being made into the Disney princess of their choice, with specific hairstyles and glitter. They all wore permanent grins on their faces, and some of them even squealed intermittently throughout the process.

The fairy godmother asked Elsa questions about the Disneyland rides and which movies were her favorites. She answered each question politely, but as she did so, I realized something. The girl who had been so excited when we entered the Boutique now looked uncomfortable. There were even moments in which she looked apprehensive—like she couldn't wait to get out of there.

I was so confused by Elsa's behavior. She spent so much of her four-and-a-half-year-old life pretending to be the "real" Elsa from *Frozen*. I thought that this would be a dream come true for her.

Then, I remembered something.

The day before, we had gone to Disney's California Adventure for the first day of our two-day pass. We decided on that schedule because it was only possible to meet Elsa from *Frozen* (and Anna and Olaf) there—not at Disneyland. Since this was her number one priority, it was the very first thing we did when we entered the park.

After waiting in line for almost an hour, it was finally our turn to meet both Elsa and Anna. She wore an Elsa costume dress that day, and her hair was somewhat grown out. Even before her glittery makeover, she still looked like a girl.

But, she looked like a girl who was nervous walking up to meet them. I even became a little nervous for her.

It was finally our turn to meet the characters, and they greeted Elsa with the kind of happy enthusiasm one would expect from them, but my Elsa was almost completely silent. Her cheeks were slightly flushed. After about five minutes, it was time for us to go. Anna then asked her a question.

"What is your name?" Anna asked.

Elsa hesitated for what felt like hours and finally spoke.

"Charlie," she said softly.

I saw a brief look of confusion flash across Anna's face before she turned toward the camera for the final picture.

To this day, I'm still not sure she even heard what my baby said, but I did. My heart broke for her in that moment. I was so sad that she didn't proudly look at each of them and say something like, "*My* name is Elsa, too!"

I was supposed to protect her, and in that moment, I felt like I had failed.

"Honey, why did you say your name is Charlie?" I asked her as we walked away.

She paused again.

"I don't know, Mommy," she finally said. "She was the real Elsa."

But my daughter was the real Elsa too. I wanted her to feel that way.

In the boutique, I started to see that this was another moment in which she felt uncomfortable. I thought I was giving her this amazing experience, but she wasn't enjoying herself the way I imagined she would. I looked to Brian for insight, and he had a horrified look on his face. I knew we would have a lengthy discussion later.

As we left the boutique, (finally!) a different child began to emerge. Rather than my sweet-natured, polite little girl, she became a diva-like, bratty child right before my eyes. It was almost like this physical princess transformation had also been some sort of psychological transformation as well.

And it wasn't pretty.

I couldn't wait to get her out of that costume and all that crap out of her hair when we got home.

After Elsa passed out in the car on the way home, Brian and I discussed the boutique experience. Just as I suspected, he didn't like it at all. We were both disappointed that we had thought we were giving her a wonderfully positive experience—one that would help transform her outer appearance into the person she already felt like she was on the inside—but she didn't seem like she enjoyed it. I might have experienced discomfort during the appointment, but Brian had experienced it even more so.

But my real question was, how uncomfortable had Elsa felt?

CHAPTER THIRTEEN

I took Elsa with me grocery shopping a few days after returning from our epic Disneyland adventure. Before we got in the checkout line, I remembered that Brian had a prescription I was supposed to pick up at the pharmacy inside the store. As Elsa and I approached, I noticed that Lyjun, my favorite Pharmacist, was working that day.

Lyjun had known us for years and was very aware that our Charlie is now known as Elsa, so it didn't surprise me when he greeted us both by name.

"Hi Tasha, Elsa. How are you both today?" He said with a smile.

"We are doing pretty good," Elsa answered in her typically precocious way.

Then she paused, because she realized she didn't know his name. She looked to me for help.

"Lyjun," I whispered to her, and she then proceeded to say "Hi Lyjun." Even at four-and-a-half years old, she was not afraid to talk to anyone.

Lyjun asked us what we have been up to, and I mentioned the recent trip to Disneyland.

"Oh, that is always a fun time," he said, looking at her then me. "Did you do anything particularly fun?"

"Yes!" I said excitedly. "Elsa went to the Bippity Boppity Boutique and had a makeover so she could become a princess for a day! They did her hair and makeup and everything! It was quite the experience!"

"Wow," Lyjun said, "that sounds really fun, Elsa. What a great experience. I bet you loved Disneyland."

Lyjun then turned away to check on the status of our prescription, leaving Elsa and me alone for a few minutes.

Elsa turned to me and in a soft voice said, "I didn't tell them, Mommy."

For a moment I was caught off guard a bit, but then I remembered the look of anxiety on her face while she was sitting in the chair and the awkwardness of the experience in general. I then realized who "them" was.

"Oh honey, what is there to tell them? You are really a girl, right?" I said to her with as much confidence as I could show her.

"Right, Mommy," she answered with conviction.

I knew I said the right thing to reassure her in that moment, but I was bothered by the fact that she somehow felt like she was keeping a secret from the fairy godmother at the Boutique.

We wanted our children to live by a code of right and wrong in their lives as they grew, but what shocked me was the fact that Elsa was showing discomfort surrounding any sort of possible deception in which she participated, even though she was only four. I was proud of her for already grasping the idea of deception, of right and wrong. At the same time, I knew I had to teach her that her truth wasn't a secret, just something to keep private. I didn't want her to feel this discomfort every time she met someone new or had a new experience.

At the Bippity Boppity Boutique, I made the assumption that since Elsa really identifies as a girl, she would absolutely love her experience there. I thought that it would be something of a rebirth for her. She would come out of the experience feeling even more like her outside matched her inside. Yet in the end, the most significant aspect of this experience wasn't that Elsa was able to further explore her feminine side, but rather that she ultimately struggled with her moral conduct in doing so. At four, Elsa was asserting herself to be a brave, confident, transgender girl, but she was showing us that she was something far more profound than just that. Not only was she hell-bent to be known as how she felt on the inside, she already knew more about being honest—with herself and with others—than some adults do. I was beginning to see that there was so much more to this story—and so much more to Elsa—than being transgender.

I paid for the prescription, and we said goodbye to Lyjun. I held Elsa's hand tightly, trying to show her comfort and support as we walked away.

"I don't want to go back to the Bippity Boppity Boutique again, Mommy," she said, keeping her gaze forward as we walked to the checkout line.

"We don't have to go back there if you don't want to, Elsa. You are my beautiful princess without all that makeup and hair glitter."

I kissed her on the top of her head and we got in line behind another mom and three kids at the checkout line.

"I'm so proud of you, Elsa," I said. She flashed me her beautiful smile that made my heart flutter every time I saw it.

Just like that, she became my confident Elsa again, with no more discomfort on her face.

For all of us who identify internally as we present to the world physically, we don't even think about some of these moments that make transgender people feel uncomfortable. We want our doctor to refer to us with the pronoun in which we prefer, and we want all of our legal and health-related documents to match our identifying gender.

Brian and I knew that we had to do everything in our power to set our child up for success, even though it seemed that she had the odds stacked against her.

I was wrapping my brain around the fact that we had to make this change legal as well. I knew several parents who had already transitioned their children and who had legally changed their children's names and genders on their birth certificates. Once I did more research, I realized how lucky we were that we lived in California. In the state of California, a person can legally change the gender on a birth certificate.

In a lot of states, this is illegal unless the person in question has gender-reassignment surgery.

Our child was too young to undergo something as profoundly invasive as reassignment surgery, but we wanted her to be respected for who she was and how she identified.

We had to do right by her. Officially making her our daughter was right in line with helping her to succeed in life.

The day we walked into the courtroom to face the judge is one I'll never forget. It was a beautiful Tuesday morning in November, and Elsa was about to turn five in a couple of weeks. She was dressed in a beautiful silk dress with horses printed on the bottom edge of the skirt. Her hair had finally grown out enough that she fully passed as a girl. We had all the necessary paperwork filled out for the name/gender change, as well as a letter signed by her pediatrician. We were so thankful that her doctor fully supported that she was an almost five-year-old child who did not identify with the gender of her genitalia at birth. We had all we needed to present to the court for the legal changes, all we needed was for the judge to sign off on our request.

When the courtroom doors opened for us to enter, my eyes flitted immediately to the judge's stand at the back of the room. The judge was a woman. My anxiety abated a bit. A woman would be more accepting, compassionate, I thought to myself. Everything was going to be okay. But I was still nervous. This was our child's legal identity on the line.

We sat down and the judge asked us why we were in her courtroom. With a wavering voice, I spoke up first. "Your Honor, our child was born male, but she identifies as a female and would like to continue to live as a female legally." I had gained confidence with every word that escaped my lips and finished the sentence with conviction. The judge looked down to assess the paperwork and then looked up to address my child. "Elsa? You feel you are really a girl, am I right?" The judge took off her glasses and patiently awaited my daughter's reply.

"Yes, I am a girl," my child responded with a confidence I had never witnessed in someone so young. My heart swelled with pride.

The judge looked down at the paperwork again and said, "Well, it looks like everything is in order. I will approve this request." Then she looked up again and said the words that will forever echo in my mind. "Have a beautiful life." With those words, a smile spread across her face.

Brian and I glanced at each other and neither of us could stop the tears from flowing. Our girl was now legally a girl.

About a week later, I was dropping Elsa off at school when another mom, Rhonda, approached me.

"Tasha! I was hoping to run into you," Rhonda started off. She looked a bit nervous, and I wasn't quite sure why. "I, uh, just wanted to say thank you. Thank you for inviting Finn to Elsa's birthday party next week. It really means a lot—to Finn, but especially to me." She paused and then looked down at her feet.

"Oh, of course," I replied. "Why wouldn't we invite him? The whole class got an invitation."

I said this like it was so obvious, knowing, of course, that this was the exact opposite thing from what we had done for last year's birthday party.

She smiled at me looking even more nervous than when she had approached.

"Well, actually, Finn has never been invited to a birthday party before."

The words felt like a dagger in my heart. I knew what she said was true. Finn had autism. Elsa had confided in me at the beginning of the school year that something was "different" about him. He made strange noises at times and had temper tantrums. He was always accompanied by a special teacher that could help him one-on-one during class. I had explained to Elsa what autism was. Finn was different, that was true, and it broke my heart to learn that there had been parties in which he was not invited because of that. That could easily have been Elsa.

I reached out to Rhonda and pulled her into a hug. She had known about Elsa being transgender since the beginning of the school year. This was our second year at that school and word has a way of getting around. A transgender child and one with autism couldn't be more different by definition. But our children had more in common than one would think. Both children might be left out of certain social events or sports; both children run a high risk of being bullied. What I had really been afraid of since Elsa had uttered the phrase at two years old, "Mommy, I'm a girl," was her being singled out for being different—by her peers, by society. I had fought so hard against the truth we now knew about our daughter because I desperately wanted her to be as like everyone else as possible. I feared her life would be so much more difficult if she presented with an identity that most people didn't understand. In that moment, I knew Rhonda previously had—and probably *still* had—those same fears regarding Finn.

My mind flashed back to Halloween, when I took the kids trick-or-treating in the neighborhood by the preschool only a few days earlier. As we approached our third or fourth house in the cul-de-sac, I saw some kids and parents from the school. I noticed Rhonda was standing on the sidewalk waving up to Finn, who was at the top of a set of stairs. He was hesitant, like he didn't know where to go, though his mother was right in front of him.

"Oh, that's Finn, Mommy. He is the kid in my class that sometimes makes silly noises, and I don't know why."

Elsa said this quietly. I was the only one who could hear her. She looked reluctant to climb the stairs. I stopped walking and turned to her.

"I know, Elsa. He has autism, remember? He's just a little different. But different is okay."

I could almost see the wheels turning inside her little head, running over the words I had just said. Her voice did not waver as she responded.

"I know, Mommy. It's okay."

She let go of my hand and climbed the stairs in her witch costume (her choice for the second year in a row) to where Finn was perched. I walked up to stand next to Rhonda. Elsa paused slightly at the top of the stairs and then I saw her lean over and give Finn a hug. He halfway hugged her back.

That was how it was—I knew he appreciated the sentiment. Rhonda had smiled at me, and I had smiled back. Elsa let go of Finn and turned around to wave at me.

As I stood there with Rhonda in front of the classroom a week later, I knew Rhonda understood this similarity that our children shared. Her embrace was tight and loving. After a long minute, we finally broke apart, our eyes misty. We nodded at each other as if to say, "I know how you feel. I got you. You are not alone." I closed the school's heavy gate behind me and walked to my car. My heart was overcome with emotion. Including Finn in Elsa's party was more than a simple invitation. It was affirmation, acceptance. It was easy. That was all I really wanted for my daughter. For her to be included, accepted. By including Finn, we were paying it forward, so to speak. I believed in karma and hoped that someday Elsa's uniqueness wouldn't just be overlooked but truly accepted by another. I knew that I couldn't change Elsa's situation any more than Rhonda could change Finn's. And now, after all I had gone through and the evolution I had seen with my daughter's transition, I wouldn't want to change her even if I could. She was Elsa, our daughter, and she was perfect.

It had taken us time to fully accept that our child was, in fact, transgender, but we were there, and we were so very proud that she was our daughter. Since her transition the previous spring, so much had happened. One of the first things I did was write a very powerful letter—which was really an ultimatum—and sent it out to everyone I knew. It was a line in the sand. Our friends could choose their side: either with us or against us. Much to my surprise, almost every single person who received the letter responded with love, acceptance, and over-the-top admiration.

"We love Elsa, and we love all of you!"

"Elsa is lucky to have you and Brian as her parents!"

"What an amazing and inspirational child she is!"

My mom's very religious cousin in Texas actually sent a card that said, "We feel for what you are going through. Love, Debbie."

She was trying.

There was only one person that hadn't responded to the letter: my cousin, Amy. I knew she was very religious. She believed homosexuality was a sin. But to not accept my child? When she was a mother herself? It was beyond my comprehension.

I feared she had decided which side of the line she wanted to stand on, and it wasn't ours. But I decided to give her a chance to explain her radio silence. Amy had just sent one of her lengthy emails updating family and friends on her one-year-old twins when I broke down and emailed her. She could send something to me about her children but couldn't seem to find the time to respond to my heart-felt letter about my own child? What crap! I was harsh in the email. I chastised her. How dare she email me about her children when she didn't have the respect to say a word about my letter—my child. I fully expected to blow up the relationship. It wasn't as if we had much of one anyway, I reasoned. We lived in different states thousands of miles away and had not laid eyes on one other in almost twenty years.

I was shocked when she wrote back the next day. She was apologetic. She hadn't meant not to respond, she said. She admitted she had been confused by what we had written and said she took time to process it all, and then time slipped away from her. Eventually, Amy said, she felt foolish and avoided me altogether. She told me she had a lot of questions to ask me, but those could wait until another time. For now, she loved me and understood why I was upset. I finished reading the email and closed it. Good. It was not a rejection. I could live with it.

I wasn't naïve to the fact that there were people out there who had different beliefs. There had already been a few people who'd had questions after our revealing letter. Some wanted to hear more scientific information, while others wanted to know how they could specifically support us and her. Some were just curious in general. One of our closest friends asked us, "Okay, so she can wear a dress now and grow her hair out to pass as a girl. But what happens when she starts to grow facial hair in puberty?" A family member had probed, "What if she feels differently in a few years and wants to go back to living as a boy?" Some of the questions we fielded were hard to hear and required us to present the due diligence of providing scientific information regarding transgender people. At certain times, we leaned on Darlene to guide us with the proper word usage to describe the process of gender transition. I vowed early on that if the person asking the question came from a place of love, I would do whatever it took to answer their question with honesty and facts. Brian and I had never even met a transgender person until we had our daughter. There were so many people out there that didn't even know what transgender meant. I didn't mind that. It gave us a chance to educate people, to show people how incredible our child was and how it was so incredibly normal to be trans. I liked a challenge.

We had learned so much in the past two years. I was so grateful to Darlene and to our support group for their honesty and their gentle push to help us transition our child, but I felt we didn't really need them anymore. At least not now. Elsa's truth had been revealed to our friends and family—we were no longer living with a secret. Brian and I were finally at ease, and most importantly, our daughter was truly happy. Though part of me wanted to see Hillary and Christy again, the other part of me didn't want to go back to the group. While it had been so helpful to be guided by these people at such a crucial time, it also represented a time in my life when I had felt so desperate, scared, overwhelmed. I didn't want to be reminded of those feelings. Worse yet, I didn't want to hear stories from people whose families were not accepting, even shaming to their child. I was in such a positive headspace, and I wanted to stay there. We could always go back later if we had questions or needed support.

I ended up needing that support again once Trump became president.

It rocked my world to the core. The cloud of bliss that I had been floating on fell from the sky and dropped me into another pit of fear and helplessness. My belief in humanity was truly tested. The day Trump was declared the winner of the Presidency, I bawled all the way to school to drop Elsa off. I could barely see the road in front of me. I'm lucky I didn't have an accident.

"Why are you crying, Mommy?" Elsa asked me so innocently.

She knew who Trump was, and to her, he was nothing more than a mean bully.

"Because Trump won, honey." I choked out the words between my gasping sobs.

Elsa's eyes remained trained on something outside the car window, and she stayed silent. When we pulled into the school parking lot, Elsa jumped out and ran ahead towards the school. I exited the car (still hysterically bawling) and made my way slowly up the front steps. Another mother was coming down in front of me.

"Oh, honey, what's wrong? Are you okay?" She asked me with concern.

I couldn't stop crying. Something told me this woman was not a Trump supporter.

"I'm just so upset over the election," was all I could manage to say.

She tilted her head to the side, her eyes displaying the same burden as mine.

"Oh, I know. It is unconscionable," she said.

I nodded my head to her, not able to say anything more, and continued up the steps in despair. I continued to cry off and on for the rest of the day.

I was crippled by the fear and anger that I felt in the election's aftermath. Our country was so divided on so many things. Again, I understood that people had different backgrounds, experiences, differing belief systems. The thing I couldn't fathom was how people couldn't accept other people. How could people want to leave others out? How could bullying those who are different be acceptable to anyone? There were groups of people—now more than ever it seemed—who were determined to keep themselves separate from anyone who was different than they were, groups divided by race, gender, sexuality, religion, etc. Those who didn't belong in the specific group were ostracized, or worse—victimized. It was all so unkind and inhumane. Inclusion of others, especially those who were different like Finn or Elsa, had so much more power.

As soon as Trump took office in January of 2017, he rescinded Federal protections for transgender people. It was literally one of his first acts as President. My worst fears had been realized. *They were coming after my daughter.* I knew that Elsa was protected where we lived in California; she could not be discriminated against just because she was trans. The law was still on her side here. But it was so disturbing and cruel that other children and adults like her across the United States didn't have the same rights anymore. Shortly after removing Federal protections, Trump also banned trans people from serving in the military. He clearly had it out for this marginalized group. I didn't understand why. It wasn't their fault that how they felt on the inside didn't match how they appeared on the outside. They were being systematically punished for something they didn't choose and couldn't control. I was apoplectic.

Instead of reaching out to Darlene, I texted Christy at the end of January. It had been almost a year since we had spoken at the support group. "I'm so upset about all these executive orders against trans people! What is going on? This is crazy! Can we meet up? I need to chat to someone about this." I needed to talk to someone who had a child like mine. She wrote back immediately. "I know. It is indescribable the amount of anger I have. I was hoping it wouldn't be like this. Yes, let's meet up. Can I invite Serena too?" Serena was another mom from the group.

"Of course," I said. I needed all the support I could get. We made plans to meet the next day at a new coffee shop in Little Italy.

The next day we met at the coffee shop and ordered our drinks at the counter. We looked around the small room and quickly made our way to a table outside. We needed an area where we could be further away from other customers, so we could speak freely and not be judged. As soon as we sat down, another couple walked over and took the table very near ours. There were so many other tables available, why was it necessary to choose that one? I thought to myself. So much for privacy. With the other couple in mind, we kept the volume on our conversation low at first. That didn't last long. We were so angry and upset that we couldn't help but raise our voices as we went back and forth. "It's the religious right, that's what this is. They have Trump over a barrel. I'm waiting for it not to be a cliché with religion and their disapproval of trans people. Just once!" Serena spouted off, and my eyes flitted to the people a couple tables down from us. They for sure heard Serena's comment. Too late now. "Well, our family is pretty religious, and they've been nothing but accepting of our daughter. I wish that that was the rule rather than the exception," I responded. Christy took a drink of her coffee and said calmly, "All I know is, it's going to likely get worse before it gets better. Trans people seem to be the new political target for some reason. We just have to do what we can do. March in the marches, donate to the Human Rights Campaign, vote for people who support the LGBTQ community and just continue to love our children." I looked at Serena and nodded. She was still too angry to acknowledge what Christy was saying.

Just then the people next to us got up from their table and were walking toward us. My mind started racing with thoughts: *oh god, they are Trump supporters and are going to go off on us.* Or, *they are going to preach some kind of Bible verse about saving our souls and our children from evil.* I reached the pinnacle of anxiety just as the woman reached us and placed a small envelope on our table. She smiled and walked out the side gate with her male companion.

Christy, Serena, and I stared at the little brown envelope for only a couple of seconds before Serena scooped it up and read the words printed on the back. "We overheard your sweet conversation. Your kids are lucky to have you as parents. Next breakfast is on us. Keep supporting each other." A twenty-five dollar gift card to the coffee shop was inside. There was no signature. We didn't need to know her name. She was an advocate. That was all that mattered. Serena looked up from the text with tears in her eyes. As if on cue, Christy and I started crying too.

We knew that this was how it was going to be moving forward. For every person who didn't accept and understand our children, there would be a person who would surprise us with genuine love and kindness. We knew we had to keep our heads up and our hearts open, for ourselves and for our children.

CHAPTER FOURTEEN

We were excited for Elsa to start kindergarten. Her new school was only six blocks from our house, and it would be the first place where no one had ever known her as Charlie.

At her preschool and through Pre-K, I had generally told Elsa's story to anyone who would listen. I used it as an opportunity to educate those who were confused, but also as a tool to weed out anyone who might be firmly against our situation. But now that she was leaving the safety of the preschool, where most everyone knew her and accepted her, I was unsure how to incorporate new people into our orbit. With this change in schools, Brian and I had to change our disclosure of her identity.

I made an appointment with Darlene a few weeks before the start of kindergarten.

Darlene greeted us with a huge smile as we walked into her brightly lit office in the back of the Victorian house. "Hi, you guys! How are you? How is Elsa? It has been a while!"

It had been a while since we had seen Darlene. We hadn't really needed to talk to her lately—Elsa was legally female and extremely happy, our friends were accepting, and there was no shame in our daughter's life.

"Oh, we are great. Elsa is great," I replied, mimicking Darlene's beaming smile back to her. "We just have a couple of questions, that's all."

Brian and I sat down across from Darlene on the green velvet couch, and I launched in. "Well, first of all, Elsa met a new friend over the summer, a girl from her art camp, Susie. She's very nice and so are her parents." Darlene was nodding her head and still smiling, waiting for me to get to the point. "Anyway," I continued, "Susie invited Elsa over in a couple of weeks for a sleepover for her birthday. I guess, I don't know. I mean, she has been on many sleepovers, but with her best friends Sophia and Ashley only. They've known her since, you know, before." I stopped to take a breath and Darlene interjected.

"What exactly are you worried about with this new family?" Darlene asked us flat out.

I looked over to Brian, and he nodded at me to continue. "Oh, well, I guess what I'm asking is, do I tell the family that Elsa is trans before the sleepover? They have no idea."

Darlene frowned slightly and crossed her legs before she spoke. "Tasha, let me ask you something," she said.

I nodded for her to go on.

"If Oliver were going on a sleepover, would you talk about his genitals with the family he would be staying with?"

Brian's face flushed red. I didn't expect her to ask something like this and, clearly, neither had he. Oliver was only two and a half and nowhere near ready for a sleepover yet, but I also knew what she was getting at with the question.

"No, of course not. Why would I mention his genitals to anyone?"

Darlene smiled again. "Well, why would you mention Elsa's genitals to anyone then?"

"So, they don't have a right to know?" I asked her, needing to hear what I knew she would say next.

"No, they do not. It is none of their business. And Elsa has the right to her privacy. This is something you must consider too when thinking about discussing her gender identity with anyone new."

Elsa's right to privacy. I honestly hadn't considered that much up to this point. She was a small child and unaware of any possible negativity surrounding her identity. But she was her own person, and she was growing up.

"You know, as Elsa gets older, she may not want people to know she is trans. I've seen many trans kids in my practice who want to be 'out' to everyone, but so many others who prefer to be stealth. It's something to consider," Darlene was writing notes in her book as she spoke, and I wondered for a split second if she was judging our parenting choices.

I knew she was right. Brian and I were still learning every day. We were going to need guidance from time to time.

We waved goodbye to Darlene and walked down the narrow pathway to our car parked on the street. I had made up my mind on the short walk. I turned to Brian and said, "Okay, honey, so I really think we should tell the principal at the new school and Elsa's teacher that she's trans. That way, they can properly advocate for her if there is any, you know," I took a sip of air so I could continue calmly, "bullying or anything." I hated letting my mind go to the thought of my child being bullied. It was a reality I had fought hard to ignore.

Brian had been quiet in the meeting with Darlene. It was now his turn to chime in. "Yeah, I agree with that. Darlene said that any school employee we tell has a legal obligation to keep the information private, so they have to keep it to themselves, or they could be sued. But as for anyone else, I say we don't tell. Elsa is going to be six years old. I think we should start to let her decide who she wants to tell, if anyone at all."

He turned the key in the ignition and pulled the car out onto the road. This was a new chapter for our family. I was curious to see how Elsa would handle her gender identity at school with her teacher and her classmates. Once again, I had to let my child lead the way.

****

On the first day of school, I asked for a meeting with Elsa's new teacher, Ms. Fox, and the principal. Both were immediately accepting and vowed to let me know if Elsa ever encountered any adversity from other students who might discover her truth. I felt supported and reassured that the school had her back.

After a couple of weeks, Elsa started to come home from school with stories about what she was learning in class, a play she was doing for performing arts, and a new girl that she really liked named Alexine.

"Mommy, guess what?!" Elsa said, bounding down the sidewalk to me one day after school and grabbing my hand.

"What, Elsa?" I asked her as we crossed the busy street.

"My new friend Alexine has the same birthday as me! November 16!"

We'd been hearing about Alexine for several days in a row, and I could tell they had become fast friends. "That is so cool, Elsa! I'm so happy you have made such a good friend. Maybe we can have a birthday party with her this year!" Elsa let out a squeal and bounced up and down on the curb.

"Yes, Mommy! I want a party with Alexine. Ask her mommy if we can do that!"

I nodded my head and smiled, wondering to myself if I should tell Alexine's mom about Elsa being trans or not. Even though Brian and I had agreed to not tell anyone new, I still had this nagging feeling in my gut about it. I wasn't sure why. As we got to our car, I told Elsa I'd check with Alexine's mom about the birthday party, and I silently told myself to wait on the rest.

CHAPTER FOURTEEN

I was putting Elsa to bed only a week later when Elsa told me she was pushed on the playground. Bedtime was often when our conversations grew deeper; Elsa asked hard questions, and sometimes her greatest fears were divulged. I treasured our bedtime conversations and what they revealed. I wasn't prepared for this one though. "Pushed? What do you mean, Elsa? Why? What happened?" Mama bear came out in full force, ready to attack any brat that had laid a hand on my kid.

Elsa remained calm as usual. "It was Annie, Mom. At recess. She said, 'you're a boy' and pushed me down."

I gasped, a little too loudly, and clapped my hand over my mouth. Annie was a troublemaker in Elsa's class. It had only been a little over a month since school had started, and it was already obvious who the problem kids were. What I didn't understand was why Annie would call her a boy. "Elsa, why would she call you a boy?"

Elsa looked down at her hands and then said, "I told a few kids in my class that I'm transgender." We had just recently started using the word transgender around Elsa. Up until then, we hadn't named Elsa's situation in front of her. Little by little as she grew, we gave her more and more information about who she was and what it meant for her future. I was surprised she was using the term with her fellow classmates.

"Oh, okay. What else did you say, and what did the others say when you told them?" I knew Annie's ultimate response, but I hoped that some of the others would have had a more positive reaction.

"I told them that I used to be a boy, but now I'm a girl." She paused and looked at me. "Jessie didn't believe me. She said, 'You are not a boy!' I don't think Duncan said anything. He just kept coloring." These reactions weren't that surprising. They were only five years old after all. What Elsa was telling them had to be very confusing. They had only ever known her to be a girl.

"What did Alexine say? Did you tell her too?" I had a feeling Alexine wouldn't even flinch, but I held my breath anyway, waiting for Elsa to confirm my hunch.

"She said, 'Oh, okay,' and that was it."

I let out the breath that I had been holding and said, "I'm so sorry Annie pushed you. That is not acceptable. I will call the school and talk to them about this tomorrow."

Elsa nodded. She appeared to be reassured, but I wasn't done yet.

"Elsa, maybe you need to wait to tell more friends at school. They have only ever known you as Elsa, so they are probably really confused." I put my arm around her and pulled her close to my chest. "And they don't need to know," I said, holding her face in my hands. "Look baby, this is not a secret, but it is a private thing. This is your information. You decide who you tell, but I want you to understand that a lot of these kids may not understand."

It was important that Elsa not feel shame. I had told myself so many times over the last few years that Elsa's gender identity was not a secret; after all, secrets make you sick. But just as Darlene had told Brian and me at our last visit in the summer, it was okay to be more private with this information.

Elsa had handled being bullied by Annie in stride. I was so proud of my daughter and how brave she already was. But truthfully, it wasn't the kids I really worried about at this age. It was the parents. What they thought and what they taught their children was what worried me. I felt like I needed an ally—not just in her teacher and school staff—but with another fellow parent.

I reached out to Nancy, the mother of a girl in Elsa's class. Nancy and I had a mutual friend whose son was trans, so I hoped that if anyone at our new school would understand Elsa as a transgender girl, it would be Nancy. I invited Nancy and her daughter, Nora, for a playdate one Friday after school in October. The girls immediately ran up to Elsa's room to play with dolls, while Nancy and I settled at the table we had outside in the sun. I wasn't ready to jump right into a conversation about Elsa being transgender, so I steered towards more light-hearted topics initially. I learned that Nora was an only child, like me. Nancy had gone to school at UCLA, and her husband was in the military. When the conversation turned toward her relationship with Serena, I decided this was my opportunity to broach the subject.

"So, I know you and Serena have been friends for several years, right?" I started off.

"Oh, yes, we met when her son, Ash, was at the preschool that I work at," Nancy replied. I knew that 'Ash' was shortened from 'Ashley,' his new name after he transitioned. I didn't know if Nancy knew that I knew this though.

"That's great," I said. "You know, I actually wanted to tell you something in reference to that," I paused.

Nancy gave me a quizzical look. She had no clue where I was going with this. Before she could ask me a question, I started again.

"Um, well, I just wanted to tell you that Elsa is like Ash," I paused again, trying to read Nancy's face. "I mean, Elsa is transgender too." I held her gaze for what seemed like forever, until she finally looked down at the table. It was just for a second and then her eyes found mine again.

"Okay. Thanks for telling me, Tasha. I accept Elsa for who she is, completely, but why, exactly, did you tell me? I'm curious." I wasn't expecting her to ask me that.

"Oh, well, I think I really need an ally at the school, you know? I mean, I have Serena, but Ash isn't in Elsa's class, so it's still a bit removed from Elsa's situation."

Nancy smiled warmly and put her hand on top of mine.

"I see. Well, like I said, I accept Elsa. Thanks for trusting me with this information."

The back door banged open as the girls ran out in their Disney dress-up clothes from Elsa's playbox. Nora was dressed in the first dress we had ever bought Elsa, the purple Rapunzel dress. Elsa was in her namesake Elsa from *Frozen* dress, her favorite garb of over a year. I had to stifle a giggle as they bounded down the stairs to us. Our conversation came to a quick end with the girls' entrance, but I had accomplished what I had intended with Nancy.

As quickly as I had been reassured by Nancy and her support of my child, I was just as quickly dismayed. We were texting about a week after our visit, and I told her about the meeting we had with the principal regarding Annie pushing Elsa on the playground a couple weeks prior.

"How did it go with Principal Elaine?" Nancy texted me.

"It went well. She spoke to the parents and assured us it won't happen again." I typed.

"That's good. And hey, I sometimes volunteer for recess duty at the school. If I ever see something like that again, I'll let you and the school know asap." I texted back a heart emoji. I got busy with work, and it was a couple hours before I texted Nancy again, this time with a question.

"Hey, did Nora ever say if Elsa told her she was transgender?" I typed the question with ease. I assumed she would write back quickly, saying something like 'Oh, yeah, all good!'

I saw the dots form on the screen and then disappear. This happened a few times. She was deciding what to type. I didn't understand what was taking so long. It was a yes or no question.

Finally, some words appeared on the screen. "No, Elsa didn't say anything."

What had taken her so long? Why did it look like she was really thinking about her response?

Then she wrote more. "Also, do we really need to use the word transgender with them? They are only five. Can't we just let them be? I support Elsa one hundred percent, but I'm not sure I want to use that term with Nora."

My heart sank when I read the text. She didn't want to use the word transgender. Didn't Nora know that Ash was trans? I had assumed she did. I guess I had assumed wrong. Nancy had assured me that she accepted Elsa, but it still cut like a knife that she was unprepared, unwilling even, to talk to her daughter about what being transgender meant.

I knew that the topic of a transgender child was a complicated one. Most people had lots of questions. I also understood that it was a difficult topic for children, but it didn't have to be. There were ways to explain what being transgender meant to a small child without too much hand-wringing.

I chose not to press on further with Nancy and her choice not to talk to Nora. I was disappointed, and I didn't feel like I should have to convince her. In our experience, kids were pretty accepting; it was the parents who ended up making things a big deal.

Darlene had helped us with how to communicate to small children on the topic of transgender. It was how our friends could tell their children and how we would soon start off telling Oliver about his sister. A parent could say to their child, "Elsa's parents thought she was a boy when she was born, but they were wrong. She is really a girl." Or, "Elsa was born with boy parts, but she is a girl in her heart and her brain." It didn't have to be complicated. But I knew that there were still many parents that simply didn't want to have this type of conversation with their children for various reasons. It made me sad. I still ached to have another family at the school that accepted and loved Elsa for who she was and talked about it openly. With Elsa's birthday approaching rapidly, I wanted to give Alexine's family a try. We were, after all, planning a birthday party for the girls together. This was the perfect opportunity to open up to them more.

I sat down a week before the party and typed up an email to Estelle, Alexine's mom. "Hi Estelle, I'm really looking forward to the girl's party at Jump Around next Saturday," I began. "I just wanted to reach out and talk to you about something a bit private beforehand." I proceeded to tell her how this was probably totally out of the blue for them, but I wanted them to know the truth about Elsa because Alexine had quickly become her best friend at school, and we wanted to make sure the family was on board. I didn't come right out and say it, but I implied that I wanted to make sure they accepted Elsa as a transgender person. I wrote the email on Saturday morning, and by Sunday afternoon I was a wreck with anxiety. I hadn't received a response from Estelle. My mind was racing. What if they were super conservative and thought being trans was a sin? What if Alexine was forbidden to be Elsa's friend? I couldn't relax. I checked my phone every thirty minutes. No email.

Finally, Sunday night at nine p.m. an email pinged on my phone. It was from Estelle. My heart leapt into my throat. Well, here we go, the moment of truth. There are only two ways that this could go. I clicked on the email and began to read. I was a couple of sentences in when the tears started rolling down my face. The email read:

> Hi Tasha and Brian,
>
> Thank you so much for sharing Elsa's story with us. Elsa radiates strength and confidence and that's because of the two of you and listening to your hearts to guide her in the direction she identifies with. Alexine cherishes Elsa's friendship tremendously. They have a strong connection like two peas in a pod; one I cannot recall having at that young age.
>
> The two of us had a good conversation with Alexine this evening about being transgender which I believe provided a lot of clarity in her little head. Alexine must have overheard other conversations with classmates because she knew Elsa

> was transgender (or as she said transporter) but did not fully grasp what that meant. She remembered the little girl, Coy Matthis, a story in her *Rebel Girls* book, as being born a boy but felt she was a girl in her heart and brain. I asked her if Elsa had given her the girl's name in the story, but she remembered from when we read it over six months ago. She decided to read us all the story at bedtime.
>
> You have our full support and hope to see the four of you soon if we don't see you at Amelia's birthday party this weekend.
>
> See you soon xoxo
> Estelle and Chris

I was overjoyed and speechless.

In Alexine's family, we had found our allies. My heart was so full, and my mind was more at ease. This kind of unconditional love for my child gave me peace.

CHAPTER FIFTEEN

When Elsa was about to turn seven, I got a call from Christy, the leader of the parents of transgender kids support group. It had been a couple of years since Brian and I had attended any meetings. Christy wanted to know if I would be one of the new parent leaders.

"You have been on this journey for five years at this point," she said to me over the phone. "I really think you have some great experience to draw upon with these newbies. You can really reassure them and help put them on the same solid path to acceptance."

She was right. I was ready to help others on their journey. Elsa was happy and confident. Our family and friends fully accepted her as transgender, apart from a few fringe people we rarely saw. We had been so lucky not to have experienced much negativity along the way. I knew that that wasn't the case for so many other families with trans kids. So many trans kids were shamed by family members, friends, schools—and they suffered a lot of anxiety because of it. If there was any way that I could show other families that they were not alone on this journey and that it truly does get easier, I was willing to try. I signed up for the following month to be the group's leader.

The group met on a Sunday afternoon in the park. The meeting location was kept private and only given to families of transgender kids by another trusted group member or a therapist. (Sadly, we knew that the group could be a target for harassment if the location were made more accessible to the public.) It was comforting knowing that everyone could share their stories in a safe place among others who faced similar challenges.

I set up a chair and a table with snacks and waited for others to appear. The group members slowly started to arrive, and it was a diverse bunch. There was an older trans man that had been an original leader of the group, a man and woman with a grown trans daughter, a lesbian couple, and a few moms who were solo. One of the solo moms had a deer-in-the-headlights look on her face and circled the group a few times, appearing very hesitant. I walked over to her tentatively and said, "Are you here for the group?" It was kind of a code. I didn't say "transgender kids group" because there weren't just families with trans kids that needed a support group. Some kids were non-binary or gender fluid. Some families weren't quite sure how their children identified; they were still trying to navigate through the confusion and fear. "Yes," the solo mom said, "I'm here for the group. I need to talk to someone… I just don't know what to do..." She trailed off while her eyes continued to dart around the park, not making eye contact with anyone. I calmly grabbed her hand and said, "It's okay, you found us. We are all here to talk—and to listen. You're not alone." I said the last part as I gestured to the group and several parents nodded their heads. The mom smiled slightly and moved closer to the group.

We all formed a circle with our chairs or blankets and one by one introduced ourselves and who our children were—basically why we were there. I started the introductions, welcoming everyone to the group. "Hi everyone. My name is Tasha, and I have a seven-year-old trans daughter named Elsa. We've been on this journey since she was about two and a half. It's been a wild ride, and she has taught us so much. I remember being very confused—sad, even angry in the beginning. This group helped my husband and me so much at that time. I learned to trust my 'mom heart' or my intuition, really, when it came to Elsa. I knew in my gut who she was even though I tried—unsuccessfully—to deny it for a while. We've all been there." I looked around the group to see some head nods in my direction. "But to be honest, we haven't been back much over the last three years because everything has been pretty steady. No bumps in the road, so to speak. I wanted to be here now to help anyone that might have some of the same questions that I did way back then. I wanted to reassure any of you that it does get easier." After I finished speaking, I passed the introductions off to a woman named Lucy on my right who told the group about her six-year-old non-binary child.

Michele, the mom with the deer in the headlights look, was last to speak, and what she said made my heart break. "Well, first of all," she started off so quietly I had to ask her to speak up. "Oh, sorry." She raised the volume slightly and continued. "Um, my son Jacob has been telling us since he was about four—he's six now—that he's really a girl. I could see it right away. He always gravitated towards the female characters in any movie and in imaginary play. He now wants to be referred to as Jessie." She squirmed in her seat after saying this, and I could tell she was getting more and more uncomfortable revealing her private information. I reached over and put my hand on her arm, since she was sitting next to me. "It's okay, Michele. We all have similar stories. You are not alone." I nodded, urging her to go on.

Michele cleared her throat nervously and continued her story. "The thing is, I know she is really that… a she. I get it. I see it. I feel it in my heart. I'm the mom. Like you said, Tasha, it's my 'mom heart,' it just knows." I had used this terminology when it was my turn to speak. I had read it somewhere along my own journey. It basically referred to a mother's intuition. We just *knew* what was up with our kids, regardless of how foreign the concept might be. I nodded, and Michele carried on. "The problem is, er, the reason I'm here is because of my husband. He just doesn't believe it. He keeps calling our child Jacob and referring to her as a *he*. I see the light in my child's eyes extinguishing every time he mis-genders her. I don't want my husband—James, that's his name—to break her spirit. He's essentially shaming Jessie. And I feel myself pulling away from James too. How can I be married to someone who doesn't accept how our child identifies and who ultimately shames her?" Michele's voice was louder now, and her anger was palpable. Before I could interject, Michele spoke again. "Worst of all, Jessie is showing signs of extreme anxiety and even depression. I'm so scared for her. I'm not sure what to do." Michele started crying then. Tracy, a mom on her other side, reached up and put her arm across Michele's shoulders to comfort her.

Michele's confession was so hard for me to hear. I had not experienced any of this type of turmoil in Elsa's journey. We had been confused in the very early stages when Elsa was between the ages of two and three or so, but unlike James, Brian had been on board as early as possible. I made a mental note to thank Brian again when I got home. His support of Elsa had helped her—and me—more than I could even describe. Anxiety and depression caused by shame would be hard to conquer, especially for a child. The group encouraged Michele to get counseling—for herself and for Jessie. We hoped that someday in the near future, she would be able to convince her husband James to come to a group meeting with her.

I looked around the group and realized that the challenges that most of these parents were facing currently were in dealing with their own insecurities or their children's. Most of them were working through issues that our family had already dealt with several years ago. I was glad to be able to be there to mentor them through these obstacles and to help them to find peace and acceptance along the way.

Just because we no longer had the same challenges as the other parents in the group didn't mean that we were past all the challenges of raising a transgender child. I was not naïve to the fact that Elsa was bound to encounter people who didn't accept her, or what I really feared—some who would even challenge her right to existence as a trans person. There was so much hate and fear in our country, and the LGBTQ community was often a target for all that vitriol. There would likely be more legislation proposed to limit the rights of trans people. It had happened with the homosexual community, and some of those infringements remained. Those thoughts were what kept me up at night. I knew that education was key. The more people that understood that gender was in the mind, the better off trans people would be. I knew that the more people I could tell Elsa's story to, the more people would understand transgender children.

When Michele had finished sharing and had calmed down a bit, I decided to speak up again.

Something specific had been bothering me for the past few months, and I wanted to get the group's read on it. "So, I wanted to run something by you all." All eyes focused on me and waited. "We have an amazing group of friends. They are all super supportive and loving and accepting of Elsa. That's not the problem. The thing I'm wrestling with is that these same friends, who seem to be supportive, haven't had any type of conversation with their own children about Elsa and what it means to be transgender. I get it for the four-year-olds, but I'm talking about eight- to ten-year-olds. It's weird. Like they are trying to avoid it. 'It's good enough to show my acceptance as an adult, but I don't want to have to discuss this topic with my children.'" I paused and looked around the group. "Is that really acceptance in the end? What are they afraid of? I can give them talking points that would make it age appropriate. I guess I'm just frustrated."

I could tell that some of the other parents were shocked that I was having an "issue". It had seemed to them that I had it all figured out. There was always something to figure out, and there always would be. We were all learning as we went along.

Tom, the elder transgender man in the group, was the first to respond to me. "Tasha, are you sure that Elsa wants those other children to know she is trans? I mean, you could be essentially 'outing' her without her consent. Have you ever thought about that?"

I looked at him with what must have been a look of confusion because he continued before I could respond.

"I'm just saying that as Elsa gets older, she may or may not want certain people to know she is trans. She may want to live a more stealth life, and if so, she may not appreciate that mom already told all these kids around her. As much as you want everyone to understand her so that they accept her, that may not be her desire."

Wow. I hadn't considered that. Brian and I had agreed to let Elsa decide whom she wanted to tell about her identity as she grew, but I had somehow not put our friend's kids into that category. Their parents all knew, so I thought they should too. I hadn't considered that I could be inadvertently "outing" my child against her wishes.

"Oh, Tom, okay, I didn't even think of this. But you are right. I do have to think about what my child would want people to know, especially in the future. Here I was kind of angry at these friends for not sharing with their kids, when really, they were doing a better job of keeping it a private thing for Elsa's sake, making her the one who should share it in the end. Thanks for helping me to see that."

Tom nodded his approval of me and then moved on to Ben, so he could share a story about his eighteen-year-old daughter and her gender reassignment surgery.

I left the meeting feeling good about how far my family had come over the years and my ability to mentor other parents moving forward. I didn't have all the answers, but with what I did know, I had been able to help others on their journeys. It was also good to be reminded that Elsa was still our guide on this odyssey, and I needed to continue to let her be.

A few weeks later at Elsa's karate class, Brian witnessed our fearless leader in action. At the end of class, the sensei had the kids sit in a circle with their legs folded "criss-cross applesauce" underneath them. Then posed a question to the group. Each child was expected to stand, say their name and age, and then give their answer. It was great public speaking practice.

Brian sat on a bench on the edge of the karate mat encircling the room with the rest of the parents.

"When it is your turn, stand and state your name and age and then answer this question: 'what is something that no one here knows about me?'" the sensei said.

Brian's eyes flicked up from his phone and rested on Elsa. He told me later that he immediately knew what she was going to say when it was her turn. His heart started racing as he tried to make eye contact with her, but she wouldn't look at him. She looked at each child as they spoke, but he said it looked like she was also thinking intently. Soon, Elsa's friend Julie stood up and said, "Hi, my name is Julie. I'm seven years old, and one thing you don't know about me is that I speak French." With a cute smile on her face, Julie sat down, and the sensei said, "Okay, thank you Julie, two claps." The kids clapped twice in unison. Two more children spoke after Julie, and then, sitting second to last in the circle, it was Elsa's turn.

Elsa stood and said, "Hi, my name is Elsa. I'm seven years old, and one thing that you don't know about me is that I'm transgender."

Oh god, she said it, Brian thought.

He looked around the room at the other parents' faces to see if there was any shock. Everyone had normal looks on their faces. No one seemed disturbed by Elsa's confession. Even the sensei took it in stride. "Okay, thank you, two claps." The sensei said that after each child spoke, the group would give two claps to the speaker and move on to the next child. Just like that. No laughter, no open-mouthed stares, nothing. Brian noticed a slight smile on Elsa's face. A sense of relief washed over him.

In the car on the way home, Brian asked Elsa about her public speaking.

"Elsa, you told the class you are transgender. How did that feel?" He looked in the rearview mirror to see her grinning this time.

"Oh, I felt proud and special, Daddy."

Proud and special. Brian couldn't wait to share this with me. Not only did the class—and sensei—take her announcement in stride, but she felt *proud and special to be transgender.* We as parents couldn't have asked for anything better than this moment.

When summer came, I received another call from Christy. This time it was about the upcoming Pride festivities. Our transgender family group was going to march in the San Diego parade. She wanted to know if our family would join. I didn't even have to ask Brian. I knew he would want to. It was going to be so empowering.

My parents were excited too, and even though the pride route was a little over a mile long, they wanted to march with us. But I still had to ask Elsa. I brought it up that night at dinner.

"Elsa, would you want to march in the Pride parade next week? It's a parade that celebrates LGBTQ people, and we will be with other transgender kids like you. Would you like that?"

Her face lit up. "Yes!" she squealed. "Can I wear transgender colors and carry my flag, Mommy?" We had amassed several trans flags over the last couple of years, and this was the perfect opportunity to wave them proudly.

"Of course, love. I will carry one too!"

My parents came over the next night for dinner, and my mom suggested we make a sign to carry in the parade as well. I got out some art supplies, and on a large piece of white cardboard, my mom wrote, "We ♥ our transgender daughter & granddaughter" in big letters. We colored the heart in the colors of the transgender flag, blue, pink, and white. My heart swelled with pride—not just for my daughter but for my whole family. We were ready to go.

The Pride Parade was everything I thought it would be and more. Rainbow and trans flags were everywhere. There were floats operated by Planned Parenthood, local bars, and restaurants, and the Human Rights Campaign. There were more floats with singing drag queens than I could count. The parade route itself was lined with hundreds of people from all walks of life. *But there are no Trumpers here*, I thought to myself. These are my kind of people. I looked over at my mom, who seemed to be taking it all in herself. Her eyes met mine, and without speaking, I could tell she was thinking the same thing—we are safe here.

My dad had brought his walking stick, since his knees had been giving him trouble in recent years. Oliver had his scooter. Mom was carrying the sign. Brian and I were holding Elsa's hands. We were ready to march. We set out on the route, and it wasn't long before tears started to stream down my face. So many people on the side of the road were yelling to us, "You are loved!" "What an amazing family!" Even, "Can we give you a hug?" As we walked, I kept looking at my family through my teary eyes. Brian walked with his head held high, like the proud dad that he was. My mom couldn't stop crying herself but was loving every minute of it; I could tell. Oliver was tooling around on his scooter with a transgender flag sticking out of his back pocket. (So cute.) My dad was hanging in there with his walking stick, determined to make it the whole mile.

As for Elsa, she was just beaming. With pride. My heart was overflowing. I knew that there would be some hard times ahead. Half of the country didn't understand or accept my daughter for who she was. But I knew that all these people at this parade—and so many more—were on our side. We weren't alone. I vowed to remember this moment when other moments tried to get me down. This moment was all about love.

EPILOGUE

I started this memoir in October of 2016. The election was fast approaching and most of the people in our orbit assumed Hillary would win by a landslide. I write in the book how devastated I was when Hillary did not win. Instead, a man who blatantly mocked disabled people and was a serial liar and cheat would become our country's next President. I remember going to bed on election night with a pit in my stomach, my mind whirling in anxiety. I had a feeling of what was to come; we'd been given warnings after all.

It was not a shock to me when one of Trump's first acts as POTUS was to strip federal protections for all transgender people and ban them from serving in our military. This meant that anyone could discriminate against trans people in the workplace, schools, and in the buying or selling of goods. Protections for the trans community were left to the states. Thankfully, we live in California, a notoriously blue and inclusive state. But now as I write this, more and more states are banning gender-affirming health care for children, and sometimes, as with the infamous "Don't Say Gay" bill in Florida, even the ability to speak about gender identity at all.

According to the Washington Post's analysis of ACLU data (Anne Branigin and N. Kirkpatrick, Oct 14, 2022), 155 anti-trans bills have been introduced in state houses in 2022. (ACLU data as of Oct 13, 2022). This means that more legislation has been filed to restrict the lives of trans people in 2022 than at any other time in US history. Trans youth are the most frequent targets of these bills. Some bills aim to restrict trans girls and women from playing on female sports teams. Others are trying to bar trans youth from accessing the bathroom that aligns with their gender identity. The most dangerous bills aim to prevent gender-affirming medical care. Arizona, Texas, Arkansas and Alabama have passed extreme bills to prevent gender-affirming health care for trans youth. This means that if Elsa lived in any of these states, she would be forced to go through puberty as a male. It would be devastating for her. Imagine being forced to live and present as the gender you do not feel that you are. So even though Trump is no longer President, the attack on transgender people rages on. Some of this vitriol is fueled by actual hate. But mostly, I feel it stems from misinformation and fear.

When Brian and I were trying to understand what was happening to our child, we did a lot of research—and continue to do so as time goes on. One of the most interesting points I ultimately read was regarding the estrogen receptor pathways in the brain. Dr. J. Graham Theisen, obstetrician/gynecologist and National Institutes of Health Women's Reproductive Health Research Scholar at the Medical College of Georgia at Augusta University talked about discovering twenty-one variants in nineteen genes in estrogen signaling pathways of the brain that are critical to establishing whether the brain is masculine or feminine. In other words, what he meant was that these genes are predominantly involved in estrogen's critical "sprinkling" of the brain right before or after birth, which is essential to masculinization of the brain. (JagWire, Toni Baker, Feb 5, 2020). Dr. Theisen's research partner, Dr. Lawrence C. Layman, chief of the MCG Section of Reproductive Endocrinology, Infertility and Genetics in the Department of Obstetrics and Gynecology, had this to say: "It doesn't matter which sex organs you have, it's whether estrogen, or androgen, which is converted to estrogen in the brain, masculinizes the brain during this critical period." What these doctors were essentially saying was that Elsa's brain was not masculinized with estrogen at a critical time in her brain development. Therefore, her brain was formed as feminine, though her body parts were anatomically male. They don't match.

What I want people to understand is that being transgender is not a choice. Elsa is not simply choosing to be female. Elsa is a "girl in her heart and her brain." It is fascinating and confusing, but then science can often be just that. When Elsa was in pre-K, she and I went to a movie at our local theater with her school class. The movie was an educational film about sea life. One of the fish featured in the show was the Asian Sheepshead Wrasse. This fish has the ability to switch its gender! Scientists believe that it likely swaps because it can pass on more genes as a male.

Elsa is now a middle schooler in the fifth grade. She is a red belt in karate, loves surfing and the ocean in general, and has her own macrame business. She is an honors student and reads well above grade level. She is wise beyond her years and always has been. Her compassion for others, including those who don't accept her, is one of the most remarkable things about her. I learn from her daily and am always in awe of her strength and her resilience. She is my hero. I hope for a beautiful future for her, one where she is not singled out, stifled or restricted. I want her to live in a world in which she can always be herself, and she can always love whomever she wants. I wish for a more open-minded world and for people to be as compassionate to her as she always is to everyone else.

I celebrate the small wins, whenever we can get them. When I have a conversation with someone who has never met a transgender person before and I see that light bulb go off in their head, I feel good. When I can impart information to someone who has a sincere question about transgender youth, and I see that they understand better than they did before, it's a good day. Elsa has already changed so many people's minds and lives. Just by existing as she is, she has helped the collective mindset around trans people move forward in a positive way. One of the most reassuring instances of Elsa's positive impact on others came from Brian's family. Brian's brother-in-law, Andy, wrote the most amazing email to me when I asked him to tell me how Elsa had changed his family's minds, and essentially their lives. He wrote:

> I would say that we found the letter you and Brian sent to family and friends to announce and explain Elsa's identity to be deeply honest and emotionally real.
>
> I realized my niece would be the first transgender person I know and wanted to understand her world better. In addition, as a part of the Evangelical Christian community, I wanted to be better prepared for discussions with fellow Christians about compassion, love, and acceptance of those who find themselves to be transgender. I did some reading from a Christian Clinical Psychiatrist with relevant experience ("Understand Gender Dysphoria: Navigating Transgender Issues in a Challenging Culture" by Mark A. Yarhouse, Intervarsity Press, 2015) and then, whenever I have found myself in a discussion where friends or fellow Church members have brought up the issue, I have taken the initiative to share my understanding of Elsa's story—specifically how she had a distinct understanding, unprompted from any outside influences, from a very young age that she was female. I often accompany her story by pulling out my phone to share a photo of Elsa to introduce others to someone who may also be the first transgender person they have personally known about. The discussion then turns to the idea that God created Elsa just exactly the way she is. And if that is the case, my understanding is that Jesus would relate to her in a way that values her soul over her body parts

> and would want to be in a relationship with her. And like all others, she is fully deserving of all the dignity, compassion, and respect available from Christ's followers and not to be dismissed with short quips or slogans seemingly designed to shut down conversations that make some uncomfortable.

We are so lucky to have the family and friends that we have in our lives. Elsa is surrounded by so many people who love her. I wrote this book with the hope that others will know her and love her too.

Once you know Elsa, there is no other choice but to love her, exactly the way she is.

ACKNOWLEDGEMENTS

I started writing this book at the end of 2016, right before the election. I didn't realize how much I would have to rely upon my own strength and the support of friends and family to keep slogging through the depressing daily news and write about my unique and beautiful child. At times it felt like the weight of the world was on my shoulders and family. But I was constantly encouraged to keep writing, re-living my memories of her birth, transition, and acceptance. I couldn't have made it through these past seven years without so many amazing people.

I am beyond thankful for my hard working and detailed editors, Neil Gordon and later Rachel Needham. Without their immense talent and tireless efforts, I would not have been able to bring this story to the world. I'm equally grateful for the extraordinary team at my publisher, Merack. Kelly, Emma, and Ashley were amazing every step of the way. A special thank you to Krista Clive-Smith for embracing my story and guiding her team to bring it across the finish line.

My mom, an avid reader herself and from whom I inherited some of my writing skills from, read and re-read my story over the years, always providing objective advice, even when it was difficult. She and my dad have always given me their unconditional support throughout my life and are doing the same for my daughter. I wouldn't be the mother I am without their example of love and acceptance to guide me along the way. I also want to thank those friends and family members who cheered me on as I wrote, always asking how the book was coming, long after many had already forgotten. A few friends read my manuscript and offered sincere advice. Thank you to Erin Braly, Carlee Gerardi, and Victoria Cole for taking time to do read throughs and to help sustain me through the writing process for so long.

I am immensely grateful to the friends and family who have loved and accepted Elsa from day one. Without your grace and compassion this process would have seemed almost insurmountable. To feel your love and support gives me hope and gets me through the day. Jinger and Geoff Ellis, Victoria and Lance Cole, Kelly Hinch, Carlee and Steve Gerardi, Chris and Estelle Truxal-Pavis, Cara Williams, Erin Braly, Aaron and Courtney Cribbes, Maria and Terrence Hiesel—thank you. To my son Oliver, who at eight is already well educated about what it means to be LGBTQ and takes it upon himself to educate his friends about acceptance and to promote anti-bullying at school. His innate compassion for others inspires me and gives me hope for the future.

It goes without saying that all our doctors and therapists along the way were essential to our process and will continue to be as time goes on. To Darlene Tando, Cristy Mereles, Dr. S (may he RIP), Dr. Jo, and Dr. G., words are not enough to express our immense gratitude.

There truly aren't enough words to describe how wonderful my husband has been over the years. Forever the calm to my storm, he has always lifted me up when I felt that I was down for the count. He has never wavered in his support of Elsa, changing course and embracing being a 'girl dad', truly believing it was always meant to be this way. He inspires me that men can be just as sensitive, compassionate, and accepting as women tend to be. You are my rock Brian, and I couldn't do life without you.

Lastly, but most importantly, there wouldn't be a story without my Elsa. I have never met another human being so self-aware and intuitive. Even when she is sad, she takes life head on, barreling through her challenges with a courage that I have never witnessed in someone so young. She is truly my Hero and I genuinely believe she will change the world. Being her mother is the reason I was born.

ABOUT THE AUTHOR

Despite her small-town upbringing in Nebraska, Tasha Kuxhausen was destined to break the mold. She is a necessary and a compelling voice for a brave new world. To her friends and family, she is fiercely loyal and a champion to everyone she loves; a fighter in the highest sense of the word. After graduating from the University of Nebraska with a Bachelor of Journalism, Tasha found herself pursuing a long career in the wine industry, where she remains. It wasn't until she and her husband found themselves on a path of acceptance after their firstborn son announced he was a girl, that she was ready to use her writing skills. Armed with a glass of wine, computer, and the inspiration of her daughter's journey, she writes this memoir in the hopes of sharing her daughter's courage and to teach others to understand how a young child fights for her identity and acceptance as transgender. As a first-time author, Tasha speaks with deep conviction for what's important to her. Loudly sharing her story to the world, she hopes to open eyes and minds to the transgender journey—through the eyes of a mother.

She resides in San Diego, CA with her husband, daughter Elsa, and son Oliver.

Printed in the USA
CPSIA information can be obtained
at www.ICGtesting.com
BVHW031249100823
668432BV00004B/16